Leon Rooke

SOUTHERN LITERARY STUDIES

SOUTHERN LITERARY STUDIES

Edited by
LOUIS D. RUBIN, JR.

A Season of Dreams: The Fiction of Eudora Welty
ALFRED APPEL, JR.

The Hero with the Private Parts
ESSAYS BY ANDREW LYTLE

Hunting in the Old South
CLARENCE GOHDES, EDITOR

Joel Chandler Harris: A Biography
PAUL M. COUSINS

John Crowe Ransom: Critical Essays and a Bibliography
THOMAS DANIEL YOUNG, EDITOR

A Bibliographical Guide to the Study of Southern Literature
LOUIS D. RUBIN, JR., EDITOR

Poe: Journalist and Critic
ROBERT D. JACOBS

Love, Boy: The Letters of Mac Hyman
WILLIAM BLACKBURN, EDITOR

Love, Boy

THE LETTERS OF MAC HYMAN

Love, Boy

THE LETTERS OF MAC HYMAN

SELECTED AND EDITED BY
WILLIAM BLACKBURN

With an Introduction by Max Steele

LOUISIANA STATE UNIVERSITY PRESS
BATON ROUGE

Library of Congress Catalog Card Number: 72–86497
SBN 8071–0909–6
Manufactured in the United States of America by
Kingsport Press, Inc., Kingsport, Tennessee
Designed by Jules B. McKee

FOR
Gwendolyn Hyman,
Gwyn, Trena, and Tom

I remember one time Mr. Linscott said that I never had to worry about publishing anything because if worse came to worse I could always publish my letters.

— To his wife, September 25, 1960

NOTES ON THE EDITING

William Blackburn

In this selection, from a grand total of about five hundred letters, I have limited severely the number of Hyman's early ones. A further limitation is that imposed by the size of the volume I have in mind—a book of moderate length, yet one long enough to suggest something of the man: his character, his humor, his relationship with his family and friends. My chief concern, however, has been Hyman's career as a writer, that is, his ambitions, his conflicts, his successes and failures, and his final disenchantment. Ideally, of course, a volume of this sort should be made up of whole letters. However, considerations of space and of the sometimes uneven quality of Hyman's letters have caused me to modify this ideal drastically. Indeed, many of the 147 pieces offered here are excerpts. Some of these are very brief, and a very few run as long as two pages and a half, an arbitrarily set limit.

Hyman wrote carefully in longhand but apparently at high speed on a shaky portable typewriter, seldom proofing his pages. Thus in his haste he left several hundred typographical errors in the originals of these letters. I have silently corrected them. To be sure, the difference between a typographical error and a misspelled word cannot be established scientifically. When faced with the unhappy choice of deciding whether a given error is one in typography or in spelling, I have tended to give Hyman the benefit of the doubt. On the other hand, I have left the fifty or so misspelled words—or what seem to be genuine misspellings—standing in the text without calling attention to them with the editorially patronizing *sic*. Many of these words are to be found in standard lists of frequently misspelled words. Others—these distinctions are not mutually exclusive—are words which Hyman usually, almost consistently, misspelled (*playwrite, rehersal, seperate*); still others are words which recall his distinctly Southern accent (*meaninless, futher, goverment*, or, humorously, *golory* for *glory*).

In addition to the typographical errors, I have also silently corrected several score words which Hyman used incorrectly—whether it is a mistake in grammar or in spelling or in the choice of diction is sometimes a nice point. For example, he once wrote *conscious* when the context calls for *conscience*.

Hyman was overfond of certain mechanical tags, such as *and so on, and so forth, and things like that, and stuff like that*. In several instances I dropped these from the text when I felt that they hindered readability.

To prevent misreading, I have (a) once or twice silently raised a letter in lower case to a capital; (b) occasionally added a comma or closed a quotation with quotation marks; (c) occasionally added an *s* to form a plural or a possessive, or a *d* to form a past tense; (d) several times changed the number or the tense of a verb: *had* to *have, have* to *has, are* to *is; begin* to *began*; once or twice, the verb itself: I *do* to I *am*; (e) used quotation marks to clarify a word as being the name of a short story. For example, "The Spotlight."

I have used brackets (a) to supply a word missing in the text; (b) to expand, whenever necessary, one of Hyman's abbreviations the first time it occurs; (c) to identify a person or place; (d) to correct a factual error; (e) to insert the correctly spelled word; and (f) to indicate the first time a name has been misspelled—unless the error is obvious or has been taken care of incidentally in a footnote.

Duke University
Durham, N.C.

ACKNOWLEDGMENTS

I wish to thank, first of all, those who have let me use the Mac Hyman letters in their possession: his parents, Mr. and Mrs. T. V. Hyman; his sisters, Miss Mitzi and Miss Dinah (now Mrs. Mark Waterman); his widow Gwendolyn; Mr. Bennett Cerf, formerly president of Random House; Mr. James Oliver Brown, literary agent in New York, and his colleague in Hollywood, Mr. Alvin G. Manuel; Signor and Signora Angelo Bettoya; Mr. William Styron; and Mr. Max Steele.

The shrewd suggestions of the following have made this a much better book than it otherwise would have been: the late Jessie Rehder, Mr. Robert Mirandon, Mrs. Mac Hyman, Mr. Alexander L. Blackburn, and Mr. Max Steele.

I am grateful to Mr. David McDowell, senior editor, Crown Publishers, and Professor Louis Rubin of the University of North Carolina, Chapel Hill, for having at one point renewed my faith in this undertaking.

Miss Dorothy Roberts, administrative assistant of the Department of English at Duke, typed most of the letters. Mrs. William Bailey, one of the secretaries of the department, typed a batch of late-found letters for me. I owe both of them thanks for their skill and patience. Mrs. J. Peter Reitt (née Barbara Black) expertly established a consistent text and proofed the manuscript.

The former provost of Duke University, Mr. R. Taylor Cole, was kind in granting me financial aid. Professor Lionel Stevenson, chairman of the Department of English (1964–

67), was good to arrange a semester's leave-of-absence for me. Dr. Benjamin Powell and his associates at the Perkins Library have put me very much in their debt, especially Mr. John P. Waggoner, Jr., and Miss Mattie Russell. I am also much obliged to Mr. Charles East, assistant director, Louisiana State University Press, Mrs. Joseph Porter, and Mrs. Robert Hall for their care in seeing this volume through the press.

INTRODUCTION

Max Steele

Why have these letters been collected and why should anyone want to read them? Mac Hyman's literary reputation is, at the moment, uncertain, and at best, modest, for the total body of his work is small. His published work at the time of his death in 1963 consisted of one novel, *No Time for Sergeants,* three short stories, and one article. The letters, themselves, do not qualify as masterpieces in the old genre of letters, those self-conscious literary works dear to Victorians. The man himself was humorous, gentle, and exceedingly loyal, and those rare qualities are present in the letters; but he is no Chesterfield and certainly he extols no virtues of character, no edifying manner of life.

I cannot tell you for what reason you should read them, but I would like to tell you why I have read them with intense need and am wiser for the experience. I have read this book as if it were a novel, indeed, as if it were a novel which Mac Hyman and I might have written together. I believe that every reader who has been involved in writing or with writers, in any way, will have that experience. For it is a novel with that dreadful though familiar theme which any student in literature might point out glibly and without pain: "The isolation of the artist in America today."

"The isolation of the artist . . ." is a cant phrase and has been worn smooth by dry and fashionable people over dry and fashionable drinks: but it is still valid and here pertains with accuracy. With many writers the isolation is obvious because both the man and the artist are in conflict with the world. In the life of Mac Hyman the situation is quite different: the man was at ease in his small-town world; the artist within him was a secret observer of that world and alien to it.

Even though the theme is a serious one, the dramatization of it is usually ironically understated. But sometimes the drama is drily absurd and often hilarious. Mac Hyman was a true humorist and was able to turn his gravest misgivings about himself into comedy. The plot itself is deceptively simple: a boy from south Georgia wants to write. With some difficulty, but after a relatively short apprenticeship, he writes a book and becomes, to all who know him casually, a rich and, for a while, famous man.

It sounds like a happy story of one of those enviable young men who does everything just at the time he should do it, conforming to his age and to the mores of his generation. In reading the letters, one sees that Mac Hyman, who signs himself lovingly to his family by that name they have called him, "Boy," is almost the epitome of a boy, and of even a more specialized and idealized creature, the "American Boy." He does all that an American boy born in a small town, Cordele, Georgia, in 1923, should do. He is first of all a loving son to delighted and delightful parents and a devoted brother to two younger sisters, the first who would become an actress and the last a painter.

Though very small in stature and light in weight, he is good at all sports in high school and later contends for the Golden Gloves. He goes off to a military school, North Georgia College, for the academic year 1940–41. In the fall of 1941 he enters Duke University and, except for the spring semester of 1942 (when he is enrolled at Alabama Polytechnic Institute), he remains at Duke, even during a summer session of 1942, until he begins his military duty.

Like many young men his age, he enters the Army Air

Corps in the spring of 1943 and the following year receives his commission as a photo-navigator. Soon thereafter he is overseas, in the South Pacific, based on Guam; and in 1945 it is his plane that flies over Hiroshima to take the reconnaissance photographs the day after the bomb has been dropped.

Upon his release from the Air Corps he, along with many other veterans, reenters college. In February, 1946, he is a student again at Duke University. Still in step with his generation, he marries a hometown high school sweetheart.

Out of college, he goes to New York with his bride. Here the pattern changes slightly. He works as a shipping clerk in a bookstore and writes on a novel, while his wife works as a fashion model. He becomes unhappy. They return to Georgia and study together to qualify to teach school. In the fall of 1948 they teach in public schools in St. Augustine, Florida, a job he does not like. Finally at the end of the semester he resigns his job, quitting it, as he learned later, on the same day that the principal had intended to fire him. For a week he drives a laundry truck and then for several months sells ice cream from a stand on the beach. Both jobs he likes better than teaching.

In 1949 the Hymans have their first child, a daughter, and Mac, recognizing the need for a regular salary, reenlists in the Air Force. In 1951 a second child is born and the following year he is out of the Air Force and again in New York City. These were restless years for many young fathers and veterans, and Mac Hyman's wanderings are not experiences apart from those of his generation.

In 1954 he publishes a book, No Time for Sergeants, and now his life becomes the dream life of many young men. He has a successful book, a phenomenal best-seller, that is made into a profitable play and movie. He has money and a great deal of it, enough that with care he probably will never have to work another day of his life. He has a beautiful wife, two daughters, and in 1955, a son. He has a hometown where he is known (though even his best friends had not known he was writing a book) and where he is respected by all men as a good hunter, fisherman, swimmer, surfboarder, cardplayer, pool player, and golfer. In short, in the expression of that day, "he has it made."

Soon he has a colonial house appropriately furnished, a beach house in Florida with a swimming pool, a cabin cruiser on which, with friends, he maneuvers the inland waterway from St. Augustine to Miami. He buys cars, large and automatic and pneumatic and air-conditioned for his family; small ones fast and perfectly adaptable to his own small frame and quick, nervous, deadly accurate reflexes. He has part-interest in a gun shop and in a skeet range. When necessary—and since he cannot be a writer in Cordele because he cannot accept the role there—he has, to satisfy the restlessness brought on by the desire to write, an apartment, or sometimes a room, in New York, or a country house on Long Island, or a place in Connecticut, and when he wants to go to try to write on the West Coast he takes a house there near the Pacific Ocean. He can go wherever he pleases, to Europe with his wife, for instance, or to Greece alone or with friends; and he can buy whatever he wants. He is, by ordinary standards in this country, a fortunate man. And in 1963, at the age of forty, he dies of a heart attack.

Outwardly, then, until the moment of his death, the man Mac Hyman has fared well and better than well. But what of the writer, the artist, and what of the isolation one has expected to find? From these letters we see that the writer, too, has been uncommonly lucky. In high school he finds eager readers through a humorous skit in the school newspaper. In the army he fills many of his evenings with writing to sustain him through years which for other men were tedious and boring. In college, at Duke University, he discovers Dr. William Blackburn and is, in turn, discovered by this gentle and complex man who has an unfailing eye for emerging literary talent.

In college and afterward in New York City and then in Connecticut, he is friends with a man who is to become celebrated as one of the most respected writers in the nation, William Styron, and one of the bright young men who is to become one of the bright young editors, Robert Loomis. At Columbia University, he is accepted in the novel-writing class of John Selby, and in the short story writing class of that old pro, Helen Hull, and in a course in literature taught by Mark Van Doren. When Hyman has completed the first draft of his novel, his good fortune continues: repeatedly in these letters he expresses his astonishment and gratitude over what his literary agent, his publisher, and his editor had done for him.

Then after a stimulating and enviable apprenticeship, which in law, say, or medicine, or any other profession, would be considered short, his novel is published when he is thirty-one, still a young man. The novel wins the praise of critics and writers, and even a writer whose praise he cherishes: William Faulkner. One asks, then, where is this theme of isolation? Where is the tragic defeat?

In the letters the reader can see about Mac Hyman something which no one seemed to realize when he was living. This simple fact: every word of fiction which he published in his lifetime, and the novel (*Take Now Thy Son*) published after his death, was worked on at one point or another in a creative writing class. In short, the only truly sympathetic world the artist in him found was in that artificial situation known on college campuses as "creative writing." For young students, such classes serve the important function of giving them an immediate audience, an atmosphere where their work is taken seriously, and where they can talk freely and without self-consciousness about writing. In the letters we see that the last ten years of Mac Hyman's life were spent in a homesick search for that sort of situation. For whereas the sportsman and the anti-intellectual found plenty to do to fill his days in a small Southern town, the artist was isolated.

It was the sense of that isolation which prompted me to write him from Europe when I first read, for the *Paris Review,* the manuscript of his brilliant short story, perhaps his best writing, "The Hundredth Centennial." The story captures better than any I had ever seen a summer Saturday in the Deep South. He had at that time published nothing and his name was unknown to me. But the name of the town and the state took me out of Paris to those lonely days when I was growing up in a small Southern town with no one to talk to about writing. I did not know that the manuscript had come in through Styron, and I wrote to Hyman to explain that the final choice would be with Peter Matthiessen and George Plimpton, but that he had written one of the best stories I had seen in manuscript.

In the following ten years, through letters and over cups of coffee in Chapel Hill, Cordele, St. Augustine, New Orleans, Ossining, and New York, and over the telephone to San Francisco, we talked indirectly about the subject of isolation but never directly. We talked in terms of place without saying that the geography we talked about was the geography of the soul.

More often it was in casual terms: "I got to get away from here. I'm not doing any work." "How you like it up there? Can you work up there?" He would say: "I think I might come up and rent an apartment for awhile." The letters, you will see, are full of such false moves: Mac and often his patient, and in retrospect, heroic wife, leasing houses, apartments, even motel suites, and picking up their children and necessary belongings, and moving, short distances and immensely long distances, to find that feeling of belonging which part of him had not felt since leaving the creative writing classes on college campuses.

He would say: "I need competition. If I'm around people writing, I can write. I think the secret is you've got to have somebody to write to." He would say: "If I could get my stuff read immediately, I could write, but this having to wait three weeks to see what somebody thinks about it . . . maybe if I got a job on a newspaper, then I could see next day what people thought." "I can't write in a vacuum." All of the conditions he sought are the conditions which generally are found in creative writing classes, and outside of them only in special groups in a few large cities, and nowhere else in America today.

Yet in those few large cities where a writer can find competition; an immediate audience; an intelligent, critical, and sympathetic readership; and a sense of artistic community, the literary and intellectual life seemed too artificial for Mac Hyman to accept for long at a time. Soon he would have to prove, over and over, that he was the well-adjusted man in his own hometown and he would return, keeping the secret artist silent, until that secret artist could no longer speak, until the artist almost, though never completely, lost the desire to speak. The successful man and the successful writer could not agree on a place to live on terms acceptable to each.

University of North Carolina
Chapel Hill

Love, Boy

THE LETTERS OF MAC HYMAN

*T*o his parents,* from Keesler Field, Mississippi, May 3, 1943, after he had been in the Air Corps for two months.

Dear Mama and Daddy,

. . . You asked me about the boys here, & I can say that there are far more boys here that I like than I would ever find in college. Everybody I knew well in my tent has been shipped out, but I'm running around with two other boys now who are also pre-cadets. One of them from Ala. had been written to look me up & so I knew him from the first. He & I will probably be shipped out together. The other is a boy from Valdosta. We are the only three in the squadron who are pre-cadets & naturally we are pretty anxious about the whole thing.

Of course there are lots of others here whom I know pretty well. They're all so different from the boys I have been meeting in school for the last few years. You don't find that pedantic, self-centered attitude about them that you find in college students. They're more simple & carefree—& naturally more fun. Some of them can't read or write & most of them haven't finished high school & yet I find them far more interesting than some of the intellectual book-worms I've known. . . .

Love, Boy

To his parents, from Fayetteville, Arkansas, September 29, 1943.

Dear Mama and Daddy,

Yesterday, I had my first taste of flying that I have had in quite a while—just enough to make me confident enough to

---

* Mr. and Mrs. T. V. Hyman of Cordele, Georgia, where Mr. Hyman is a merchant and his wife an enthusiast for the arts.

think I could solo at a moment's notice. We took off from the field—there was a pretty rough wind—and he carried me out to my practice area, showed me the pattern of the field, explained the layout of the surrounding country, and about a million other extremely important things that died out in my mind two seconds after I heard it. He didn't let me fly it any, though, and so I got in only 35 minutes of time—his flying and my time.

But today there is a far different story. Before this thing is over, I'll probably be a religious fanatic, myself, with the idea that if the Lord didn't give me wings, I shouldn't be trying to fly. My instructor, by this time, probably has the same idea about me.

He climbed in the plane today and told me to take over, taxi out to the field, and take off. Evidently he had forgotten that I didn't fly it any the day before—or else he is just one of these don't-give-a-damn persons who don't care much about life in the first place.

Taxi-ing wasn't much trouble. I followed the ship ahead of me easily. After all, I was born on the ground and have lived twenty pretty nice years on the ground, and I am, therefore, very much at home and very comfortable on the ground. But the instructor had different ideas & it wasn't long before he was telling me to give it full throttle. Then a little forward pressure on the stick, then a little backwards pressure and we were off to God-knows-where, wobbling like a wounded duck and ducking up and down as if it were bobbing for apples. Finally, I reached 500 ft., so the altimeter said, and I leveled off, mashed the left rudder and gave it left stick and everything on earth started leaning and I could hear strange noises coming over the earphones and the controls started jerking and suddenly I realized that the instructor did have a certain amount of respect for life after all—he was yelling at me to roll it out. Whereupon, I realized that I had a right rudder, too, and mashed it ferociously, giving it right stick. We rolled over to a position called level, which is a gross exaggeration—but it's about as near to level as I got all afternoon.

From there, I went on to the training area—still supposed to be flying straight and level. Straight and level isn't as simple as it sounds. The plane has one idea, the instructor has another, and I—well, I don't have many ideas; I [am] perfectly willing for either to have his own way just so I can tag along. The instructor would yell at me to look at my right wing. I would look at it and nod and smile. Then I would hear him yelling, "Well, do something about it!" Now, as far as I was concerned, the right wing was perfectly all right. We were moving right along, and if the right wing felt like going up and down and going into all sorts of contortions, it was all right with me. But I would pull it down to please the instructor (Mr. Lester is the man's name) and then I could hear him saying, "Now look at your left wing!" This nonsense continued all afternoon. When it wasn't the right wing, it was the left, when the nose wasn't too high, it was too low.

Then came the right turns. Right turns aren't just turning the plane to the right. You've got to establish a 45° bank, keeping the nose on the horizon, turn 90° and roll it out. It's not that simple either, but I haven't got time to make it sound ½ as complicated as it is. Once I mistook the throttle for the stick and nearly cut the engine to gliding. Mr. Lester, to show me what would result from this, put the ship into a spin, and while I was hanging on for life and getting as far from those controls as I could, he sat there calmly counting the spins. That broke me from cutting the throttle.

After several more pretty horrible turns on my part, he asked me the way back to the airport. "That way," I said, pointing—polite or not. So he told me to head it in the opposite direction and we would go in.

I landed it. I don't [know] how to write that sentence with a sigh of relief, but all the feeling you can muster up should be read into it. The landing, though the ground was rushing by as if we were skidding and wobbling all over the place, was three-point, which is supposed to be good—something like a five-star picture. I won't say it was an accident—that would be sacriligious; it was a miracle if ever one happened.

Believe me, though, I was so thoroughly disgusted with myself when I did step out on terra firma that I thought I might as well hand in my resignation with no more ado. My turns had been awful I knew. He assured me, though, that I wasn't the worst he had ever seen & that made me feel a little better—maybe I can be a bombadier.

Love, Boy

To his parents, from San Antonio, October 5, 1943.

Dear Mama & Daddy,

Today I took part of my physical and passed it all right. There was a night blindness examination and blood test and so on. Tomorrow I will complete my physical & find out whether or not I have passed.

But let me tell you about the psychiatrist. That's the thing I've been worried most about, you know. He's the one who washes you out for nerves and stability and lack of common sense & character, etc. Frankly I was scared to death.

When I finished my blood test and turned in my paper on it, the fellow at the desk turned to a captain and said, "Is this the man you wanted to see?" Then they sent me to Booth #2 and in a few minutes the captain came in. He was about forty years old and wore a foreign service stripe and could stare through you as if you were glass. He asked me a few questions about previous nervousness, etc., and then asked me to hold out my hands over the table. They were shaking as if I were in a jeep. He shook his head and said that looked pretty bad. He asked me if I had always been that nervous. I told him if I were a captain & he were a private and as much of his future depended on me as mine did on him, he'd be nervous too. And then we got to arguing. He asked me all sorts of questions—personal and otherwise. And the longer it went, the worse it looked. Finally he asked me to take my choice between aerial gunnery and O.C.S.—practically telling me that I would never be able to fly or be a bombadier or anything. I told him I was going to fly one way or the other and told him that he just couldn't wash me out after a short talk.* But he quickly reminded me that he could.

I was getting worried and mad by that time. He said he had been across and that he knew the type of men that were needed and that too many men had been sent across when they should have been washed out then and there. In answer to that, I told him I had never seen anyone that I truly feared and that I thought I could make as good [a] soldier as he ever had.

And so it went. Finally he asked me again whether I wanted O.C.S. or gunnery and took out his pen and started to write it down. I started arguing again about not being nervous and so on and then he turned around the paper and pointed to the number he had written on it—168. "See that number, son?" he asked me. I asked him what it meant—I was sure by then that I had failed. "That," he said, "is the highest mark I have ever given to a man and I've been doing this for about three years now and have interviewed plenty cadets." Hon-

* Hyman's interview with the psychiatrist doubtless suggested Will Stockdale's in *No Time for Sergeants* (New York: Random House, 1954), 102–108. Nelson Algren finds in the center of that book the idea of belonging: "Yet Mac Hyman's comedy is more than farce . . . because he has backed it with a vivid insight and a real feeling for character. . . . Where [Ring] Lardner's heroes were forever cutting themselves off from humanity, Mac Hyman's are always joining up." See Chicago *Sun-Times*, October 3, 1954, Sec. 2, p. 4.

estly, I nearly fell through the chair. I felt so sheepish and so proud that my chest would droop and swell alternately.

He went on to explain to me that he had picked me when he saw me standing out in line and had made a bet (no money involved) that I was "a superior person." (I'm not saying that; he did.) He said that I had the brains and stability (?) and everything else to get through and that I would make a "damned good pilot" as well as bombadier— and that I had picked the right thing. I don't mean to be bragging, but you can understand that I am proud of it, and I knew you would like to hear it.

He kept me in there quite a while after that—just talking to me. I was in my booth long after the others had left, and when I came out, everybody wanted to know what had kept me so long—they thought I had washed out. . . .

Love, Boy

Hyman was to be commissioned a second lieutenant in pho-to-navigation, that is, he was in charge of navigating a B-29 reconnaissance plane to a given target and, once there, he was to photograph it. The missions were of two kinds: before an air raid, to photograph the targets to be hit; after a raid, to photograph the damage done to the targets. Hyman was to fly a total of twenty-three missions.

To his parents, from Salina, Kansas, June 15, 1944.

Dear Mama & Daddy,

. . . Night before last I went on a flight up to Denver. It was the biggest mess of navigation you've ever seen. I was in a B-17 (yes, I'm still going to be on a B-29—we just train on the 17's) and in the navigators compartment in the nose of the plane, there was no compass, no calibration cards, no nothing.

In other words, what few instruments I had were very incorrect & I didn't even have a compass.* Well, by estimating & by pilotage I was able to get us to Denver pretty well, but then we started back. For a while I was doing all right, but gradually I saw that we weren't passing over the towns on the desired course. I called the pilot & asked him if he was holding the heading of 83° I gave him. So then—and not until then —did he tell me that he had changed to a course of 40° a little while ago. He didn't remember just when & having forgotten that I had no compass, he failed to notify me.

I worked furiously trying to estimate where he had changed course (he was trying to fly around some bad weather ahead of us) & finally guessed at a position. Figured I had better check up then so I called him up & asked again. Now he is on a course of 60°—still trying to get around the storm. Well, I couldn't see the stars to shoot a fix, so I tried radio. There was too much lightening for radio. Then he had nerve enough to ask me for a heading for the base—and he had flown all sorts of directions without notifying me. I didn't even know which way he had been flying much less where we were.

Well, I guessed again, gave a heading, & finally came to a town that I couldn't identify. We circled it until we were able to get in touch with a radio tower (the weather had cleared) & found that we had passed right on by the base. Well, we got back. From there, I carried them right home.

I was pretty disgusted when I got back, but the pilot apologized for not telling me when we changed headings.

Got to bed about 3 AM, got up at 5 AM. Last night got to bed about 1 AM, up again at 5 AM. & flew this morning—& did all right, I think. Might fly again this aft. but I hope not.

I don't know whether I care for this life or not. Frankly, I

* This espisode from real life foreshadows a fictitious one in *No Time for Sergeants,* pp. 148–54, when a plane is presumably lost over the Gulf of Mexico.

had just about as soon be a pvt. back in basic. I don't like this responsibility. . . .

Love, Boy

To his parents, from Guam, April, 1945.

Dear Mama and Daddy,

Tonight I'm sitting down in the Orderly Room with a pistol on my side so big that I have to walk sideways to balance myself. I'm serving my term as O.D. [Officer of the Day] and as yet have had no major rebellions or outbursts. All I do is sit around, looking omniscient, and explain to those who want to get off K.P. that I had absolutely nothing to do with putting them on K.P. and that I don't have the slightest intention of doing it for them. Also I have to go through the barracks and see that all the lights are off and that the boys are behaving like good little soldiers, and I have to break up all the wicked dice and poker games (Incidentally, I won over thirty dollars the other night.) and do my best to keep a straight face when they give me the same excuses that I was giving only a few months back. Aside from that, I have read one book and about five different magazines since I came on this morning. . . .

Love, Boy

To his parents, from Guam, April 14, 1945.

Dear Mama & Daddy,

. . . An incident happened the other day which caused me to lose the last of that small bit of respect I have for the ground men of the air corps who sit in the orderly rooms. In our outfit there is a repulsive, red-headed little varmint—now a captain—who calls himself the Adjutant & who has received his promotions thru his ability to pat the right backs at the right time. I was O.D. a few days ago when I learned that I was to be alerted the next day & would fly the next night. So I went to this burr-headed, two-barred nincompoop & asked to be released from OD as it would mean my staying up all that day, all night (you can't go to bed on OD), all the next day (getting briefed, drawing the charts up, a million other details), all the next night (as we were taking off early—possibly I could have gotten a couple of hours sleep, but I didn't), and all the following day while flying—something near to *sixty* hours up with, at most, three or four hours sleep. And that poor, silly imbecile, who has nothing more to do than sit at a desk a few hours a day, had the nerve to try to refuse. In fact, he had just begun to refuse when I turned & left him & went to see the Executive Officer, a Major, who had me relieved in less than five minutes. There are some people this army could do without. . . .

Love, Boy

To his parents, from Guam, April 18, 1945.

Dear Mama & Daddy,
 . . . Usually the nervous reaction from a mission, caused by being under a physical & mental strain for such a long time, doesn't set in the day or night of the return (for the person is still rather tense, even though exhausted) but the next day after a long night's sleep. Then a person seems rather fidgity and depressed. I've noticed it in myself. I know the day after a mission I smoke more than usual and feel pretty antagonistic toward everything & everyone. On the mission itself, though, over the target I am becoming very proud of

the fact that I can keep pretty calm and seldom raise my voice anymore than usual. I know the reason I don't get any more excited is because I am so busy concentrating on getting the target, but the crew doesn't know that & far be it from me to explain it. I honestly don't mean to brag so I hope you don't take it that way. I believe that if anyone on the crew took my job over the target & had as much to look for & think about, that they wouldn't have time to worry about other things either. Anyhow, even though the impression might be false, I've gained a pretty good reputation among some of the crew & I'd like to keep it, and even though I say it myself, I'm d—— *proud* of the fact that I don't whimper & whine as some people are bound to do. O.K., so I *am* a braggart. . . .

Love, Boy

To his sister Mitzi,* from Guam, April 27, 1945.

Dear Sister,

. . . From the letters I've received from home recently, I hardly expect Dinah† to be alive by the time I get there. In every letter Mama explains to me that Dinah has just picked up some unheard-of malady and is far too frail to go to school. In the last letter, she said that Dinah "hadn't been to school *that* week, but that she was planning to go *next* week, if the sun was out." I simply can't believe she is that bad off—especially when she can say, "I think I'll be sick tomorrow"—and the next day show distinct signs of everything from measles to epileptic fits.

Today I read *Life With Father* and got to thinking about some of the antics that the Monster [their father] goes through. You ought to read it & compare the two. I think

---

* Mitzi Hyman ("Sister"), was director of dramatics for several years at Emory University, and director of the Pocket Theater in Atlanta. Currently she is a graduate student at the University of Georgia.

† Dinah Hyman is now Mrs. Mark Waterman of Jacksonville, Florida. Before her marriage, she taught painting in the public schools there.

Daddy would come out in front in the long run. He would especially shine in such acts as tying his bathrobe to the foot of the bed & grabbing up that chair with the roller in the living room, slamming it around to face the wall and yelling that "he would swear & be damned if he could understand why nobody would leave that chair the way he wants it." You should read that, really, if you haven't already, & note the comparison.

Love, Boy

To his parents, from Guam, May 17, 1945.

Dear Mama & Daddy,
    Just got your letter telling about V-E day at home & all the whimpering that went on & I more or less agree with Daddy about staying in bed until Japan surrenders. I would have liked to have been there though. I can just imagine Mrs. —— explaining how hard the whole thing has been on her & how glad she is that it is over. I know the Church service must have been impressive though. It's funny how they can say "Thou shalt not kill!" in one breath & shout something about backing the war effort in the other. And then when it's all over everybody goes back to them [the churches] & thanks God that we were able to kill so many Germans and ask for strength so that we might kill the Japs all the sooner. I don't see how they get away with it. . . .

Love, Boy

To his parents, from Guam, May 22, 1945.

Dear Mama & Daddy,
    . . . About that "damaged" plane, I wish you would not run about shouting it all over town & making me feel like an

idiot. Most boys have taken the martyr attitude of "never telling nobody back home nothing" because they don't want anybody worrying as they are perfectly willing to bear their noble burden like strong, silent soldiers & in some cases, I guess that is the best thing to do, but I haven't done that because I know that you all are interested. But the letters that I write are to you all *only* & I'm asking you again to keep them to yourself. And if you *ever* have anything in the paper that I say, I really won't like that. I mean what I say. Please don't do it. I've read enough of other people's mail while censoring to know how silly it sounds when a person tries to give the impression that he's practically winning the war single-handed. I don't want to be put in the same position myself. . . .

Love, Boy

Ever since the high school newspaper in Cordele published a short humorous article of his, Hyman had been trying to write. By the time he was eighteen and a sophomore at Auburn—where he was encouraged by the late George Marion O'Donnell—he had narrowed down drastically the possibilities of a future career: "If I can't write, there's nothing much left I can do, I guess." See letters of January 17 and March 24, 1942, in the possession of Mr. and Mrs. T. V. Hyman.

To his parents, from Guam, July 21, 1945.

Dear Mama & Daddy,
 . . . I've been doing a bit of writing lately—a couple of hours nearly every night. Some of it comes out all right & some doesn't. I usually get a good start, get bogged down, tear it up & begin something else. I've got one going now that's doing better than expected. I think I told you about my

tentmate who was writing a book before he came into the army. He taught a while at Chapel Hill while working on his Ph.D. & he writes quite a bit here. I don't know how good he is as I haven't read any of his stuff (he mails it to his wife), but I enjoy talking to him. I think by the time I get home and finish school (if I'm not too old by that time) I'll have enough money to tide me over a year or two and I can have my fling at it. Whether or not I'll be any good, I don't know, but I've got to try. . . .

Love, Boy

On Iwo Jima, Hyman, as photo-navigator of his plane, received a mysterious order to photograph Hiroshima the following day. Equally mysterious was the fact that a plane was awaiting their return to Iwo, ready to fly the pictures of the ruined city to the United States. That evening President Truman announced the dropping of the bomb.

To his parents, from Guam, August 8, 1945.

Dear Mama & Daddy,
 . . . As we approached Hiroshima, Snow mentioned to me that it looked like a ghost city.* I said, yes, it looks even worse than Tokyo. Of course, at that time we did not know that it had been hit the day before by the Atomic Bomb that has been receiving so much publicity for the last two days. It wasn't until we got back to Iwo that we learned that we had

---

* Another version: "Just before we got there . . . I saw what I thought was a large layer of clouds ahead and thought we wouldn't be able to take any pictures. Just as we passed over, though, we had a clear view of the city and started the cameras going. . . . I turned to the co-pilot behind me and told him to look. I asked him if he had heard of a raid on Hiroshima and he hadn't either. So we flew over it, both of us leaning over and looking out at the place. It was pretty silent down there, no flacks and no fighters." See article by Marti Martain, Greenville (N.C.) *Reflector*, November 17, 1962.

taken the first pictures of the destruction it can cause.* So, just to help my ego, I can tell you that photographs that so many people were waiting to hear from were taken by us. If they happen to print any of them in any magazines, I wish you would save some for me. . . .

Love, Boy

To his parents, from Guam, August 28, 1945.

Dear Mama & Daddy,

 . . . I feel, as you do, that my job should be through, but you ought to know better than suggest that I refuse to fly anymore. You also mentioned something about not seeing why we let Japan off so light. I can't understand anybody making a remark like that. I don't call destroying hundreds of thousands of people with fire raids and atomic bombs, burning out and ruining every fair-sized city, sinking about 4/5 of their navy, insisting on unconditional surrender so that we can destroy all their war industries, destroy what's left of their navy, occupy their land for years, take away their possessions, control their trade and make over their government, letting anybody off light. Letting the emperor stay in as a puppet was a smart thing to do in my opinion. How else would we have ever gotten those armies to surrender? How else could we have made a treaty? . . .

Well, so much for that.

I've been trying to write a little more lately, but I just can't seem to get with it. I'm too restless now thinking about getting home. I did write one story, though, that seems to

---

* Hyman had no way of knowing, of course, that the plane which had dropped the bomb the previous day had also photographed evidence of its destructiveness—a column of smoke ascending 20,000 feet over the city.

scan pretty well on a second reading. It's not much good, but at least I don't rip up the paper and feel like choking myself after looking over it.

There are so many things I want to write about, but I just can't form them in any sort of a pattern. If things were written truly as they are, there would be very little pattern and very little sense to them anyhow, but it seems for things to be liked they have to be taken in even, set doses. You have to take a real thing and add a few lies here and there to make it complete and digestible, so that a person finishing it knows that everything is fine & dandy and now he can forget all about it. You have to have the bandying back and forth of smart conversation and then the final grand clinch of the lovers—it seems a rather cheap way of writing, but it seems to pay. I hope someday I can make it pay, if I can hold my stomach down to write it.

Love, Boy

In February, 1946, Hyman returned to Duke as a member of the senior class.

To his parents, from Duke University, September 26, 1946.

Dear Mama & Daddy,

. . . At first I decided to drop Philosophy, which seems to get nowhere after a lot of talking. I dropped it instead of the Greek lit. class. But then I went back to the Greek class this morning and got so fed up hearing them talk about gods and goddesses, that I went back to the office and told them I had changed my mind and wanted the philosophy. We finally worked it out. As I am not interested in either course, it was simply a matter of the lesser of two evils.

I can't seem to get down to studying. I don't expect or even care whether my marks are especially good this time. I just want to get a "C" average and get out and be done with it.

Today, though, something happened that caused me to walk on air for a few hours. I have told you of the writing class. We have about 25 students in it & all of them are supposed to be pretty good as they have to qualify to get in. Well, for last Tuesday, we had to write a short story especially concerned with sensory impressions. I wrote one, a short one, about standing behind a hill while there was fighting on the other side of it. I thought it was pretty good, but I wasn't sure.

Well, we spent 2 hours Tue. aft. in class going over the papers, criticizing them for unity, motivation, & what-not. He didn't mention mine. Then today we spent an hour at it & he still hadn't mentioned mine. Then at the last of the period he threw it across the table at me and told me to read it to them. I did & everybody seemed to like it. In fact, Dr. Blackburn went so far as to say that it was "an artistic achievement, beautifully planned and with an extremely effective use of understatement." He is usually pretty sarcastic and as he had always seemed not to like me very much (he was the one that gave me the "C" last semester) I was pretty surprised. He said that I was to be congratulated on that and had written on the back of it that I should try to have it published in the *Archive,* the school magazine. (I don't know about that, though.) After class I had several of them come up and tell me they thought it was very good & so on.

I hate to go along tooting my horn about it, but it did make me feel pretty good. I don't think there is anything that can make me feel any more pepped up than writing something and having someone understand it and like it.

I guess I'd better stop. I've told you the main thing I wanted to tell you. . . .

Love, Boy

To his parents, from Duke University, January 17, 1947.

Dear Mama & Daddy,

. . . Have been working very hard since last Saturday—every afternoon & until two & three o'clock every morning. Finally managed to turn in a 2500 word term paper, a 500 word book review, and a 6000 word short story. Had to rewrite the short story about five times (I guess I typed over eighty pages) before I got what I wanted. I think, now, it's all right. Turned it in yesterday afternoon & celebrated last night by eating a steak & going to a movie & doing nothing. Got so wrapped up in that story, I feel as if I've been asleep for the past few days.

I was telling you over the telephone that the *Archive* wanted to publish the *Dove Shoot*, but I went down & told them not to as I was going to send it off. The fellow that advised me to send it to *Esquire* is a boy who goes here & knows a pretty good bit. He has a couple of his stories in an anthology.* Dr. Blackburn said *Esquire* might be the best deal, but he wants a copy of it to send to a Greensboro contest, which is made up of some of the top critics in the country.† Anyhow, I took it away from the *Archive* to try greener pastures. If I can't sell it anywhere else, I'll carry it back & let them publish it. . . .

Love, Boy

Hyman graduated from Duke in February, 1947, but stayed an additional semester in order to continue his writing. He and Gwendolyn Holt of Cordele were married on January 31.

* William Styron, "Autumn" and "The Long Dark Road" in *One and Twenty: Duke Narrative and Verse, 1924–1945* (Durham, 1945).

† In the spring of 1947, "The Dove Shoot" won a place in the arts festival issue of *Coraddi*, undergraduate journal of the University of North Carolina at Greensboro. The chairman of the visiting critics that year was Robert Penn Warren.

To his parents, from Duke University, April 27, 1947.

Dear Mama & Daddy,

Haven't heard from you all in quite a while & have been wondering how everything is at home. Wish you would drop me a letter sometimes.

There's not any news to amount to anything. We are still getting along fine in the apartment & are much more satisfied at having a place to cook & everything. Last night we had Tommy [Fletcher] & another fellow (the one who bought us that basket) out here to supper & we had a pretty good time. Gwendolyn fried a steak & made a pie. We don't have much room up here & I had to sit on a box to eat & Tom had to sit on the bed. We eat off a card table. It was fun though. That's the first time we've had anybody up here. We felt that we had to have them because they had carried us out once before.

The writing class gave a banquet for Dr. Blackburn the other night. He was pretty pleased about it. Afterwards Dr. Blackburn, Tom [Greet],* another fellow & I went out & had a few bottles of beer—first I've had in a long time. The other fellow's wife was here at the place with Gwendolyn. By the way, Dr. Blackburn is sending three of my stories to the agent in New York this week. Don't know when I'll hear from it. He is sending "William" & two others that you haven't read. I wrote the other two in the past few weeks & he thought they were both good enough to go up there. Have been outlining a novel but am rather afraid to start on it. I know it's time I should be starting, but I just somehow don't feel up to it, don't know whether I'll ever have the patience to finish. I guess the only way to find out is to try it, though. Dr. Blackburn keeps saying that I should go ahead with it. He wants me to have in at least one chapter before I go home so I will have a start anyhow.

* Thomas Y. Greet, Duke '47, of Greenville, S.C., now Professor of English, Virginia Military Institute, Lexington.

I am still waiting to get *The Dove Shoot* back from that magazine. I'm getting disgusted with it. I want to send it to *Esquire* or somewhere. Might possibly can sell it.

I'm getting worried about what to do this summer. I feel as if I should go ahead and get a job, but still I would like to take a crack at writing for awhile & yet I'm afraid I'm just making a fool out of myself for trying it. I wish I didn't want to write so bad. I know I'll never be happy if I don't. I was thinking that I might could get a job somewhere & try to write in my spare time. Of course I can go for a while on the money I'll get from the car and had rather do that, but I hate to seem as if I am just loafing my life away. Writing to me is about the hardest work I can imagine, but nobody else can believe that. But I guess now that I've gone so long with the reputation of being a loafer that it won't hurt to go a little longer. Anyhow, I'll talk to you about it when I get home.

Write & let me know how things have been getting along. I've wondered how Idie * is doing. You ought to let me know. Going to call you as soon as this [telephone] strike gets over.

Love, Boy

To William Blackburn, from Route 3, Cordele, Georgia, June 23, 1947.

Dear Dr. Blackburn,

Got the stories you sent back a couple of weeks ago and I want to thank you for giving it a try even though it didn't work out. Of course I was a little disappointed over it but I didn't let the criticism bother me very much as I more or less dismissed the whole thing from my mind when Mr. Shaeffner

* Hyman's Aunt Idie, Mrs. Ellen H. Johnston, lived with his maternal grandmother, Mrs. Nell Forrester Hooks, in Leesburg, Georgia. Mrs. Hooks has since died.

[John Schaffner, literary agent in New York] insisted on calling them "sketches." That gave me the loop-hole I've been crawling through since that time: I tell myself that he just simply didn't understand them. Anyhow, it makes a good alibi for myself.

I appreciate your sending the list of magazines along. So far I've sent "William" to *Esquire* & it has been returned. They said it was too long—they like stories less than 3000 words—that it took too long in getting started (which is probably correct), and that they don't favor stories told in the first person anyhow (which confirms my opinion that Mr. Farley was probably right in having *Esquire* banned from the mail.) I also sent "The Bus Going Home" and "Wind in the Trees" to that Atlantic "First" Contest, magnanimously telling them to take their pick. Then I sent the one called "Aunt Jessie," which you might possibly remember, to *Collier's* (getting more brass every day) which I haven't heard from yet. I don't have any hopes on that, though. My excuse is I did it to please my wife.

Other than that I have written three chapters to a novel, centering around the boy Paul,* which so far seem to reach some sort of new low in writing, and one chapter to another one which I turn to when I become sufficiently bored with the first. All in all, I seem to be beating my head against a cement block which shows no indication of cracking. So much for the work—

We are looking forward to your and Tom's visit.† It's pretty easy living out here if you want a rest, fishing and swimming a little and a place up the road where you can get beer. Let us know when you're planning on coming down. We don't have Tom's address and haven't heard from him

* Probably the beginning of *Take Now Thy Son*, published posthumously in 1965 by Random House.
† Tom Greet and I visited the Hymans in their cottage on Flint River, about ten miles south of Cordele, in late July.

since being here. Hope your teaching job in Tenn. comes out all right.

We are planning on your coming down so don't disappoint us. I'll let you know if I have any luck with any of my stuff.

Sincerely, Mac

To William Blackburn, from Route 3, Cordele, September 9, 1947.

Dear Dr. Blackburn,

. . . The situation is this: I haven't written a worthwhile thing this summer; I haven't published anything; I can't even turn out a good enough story to send to that man on the *New Yorker*; and what's worse, I'm getting to the point where the whole thing seems useless and I keep worrying about every story's worth before I even finish it. As you know, the three different attempts I've made at novels have turned pretty stale within a short time. I don't know exactly what I can do about it, but I've got to do something.

For awhile I considered going back in the army. I thought that maybe then I could have plenty of free time and a little variety that would keep me from getting so stale. I even went over to Montgomery to fill out the papers & then changed my mind. I tried for newspaper jobs in Miami, Macon, Montgomery & several other places & there doesn't seem to be much doing there. So I have finally narrowed my own weak-faced alibi down to this: The reason I am drying up around here is that I don't have any feeling of ever accomplishing anything. I know that sounds awfully trite, but it is the truth—at least, part of it. When I was at Duke, I could write a story and get a certain amount of interest from the class and from you, and then I was very excited about the thing and was eager to start on the next one. That kept me going pretty well for a time.

But here if I don't publish a story, I feel that it is an utter flop, which most of them [are] beginning to be, and that the whole thing has been a waste of time. And I'll swear and be damned if I can write anything decent as long [as] I sit around questioning myself on "Will they publish this or is this a waste of time, too?" In short, I get so frustrated I feel like exploding all over Cordele, and I think it [is] time I started getting out.

So what I wanted to ask you was if you know of any place—any kind of school or community or anything—where I might could go so that I could at least be around people that write and take an interest in such things. I don't know that changing places to live would help matters, but I'm willing to try it. I guess I need somebody to push me, being as I don't have the guts to do it by myself. I was thinking that you might know of some place where you could enter under an instructor's guidance and maybe sit in a class or something. I would like to try anything like that—anything but what I am doing now. I read of one fellow out in Oklahoma who is supposed to take in groups of that sort, but I learned later that it was a home-study course which I don't want. I also heard there was something like that at Columbia University, but I don't know. I hate to think of going to school for the rest of my life, but if that is the only way I can get anything done, I think I had better try it.

I'm sorry I have to keep bothering you for help, Dr. Blackburn, but it seems I can't make my way without it. I really would appreciate any suggestion you might have.

Sincerely yours, Mac

P.S. *The New Yorkers* turned *The Dove Shoot* down, but wrote me a nice letter and asked for some more. At least, that's better than the usual rejection slip.

To William Blackburn, from Route 3, Cordele, October 5, 1947.

Dear Dr. Blackburn,

I got your letter today and want to thank you for all the trouble you've taken with me. I called Mr. Selby in New York just after I got your post card, and he told me that the class was already over-crowded.* He was very kind about it, though, and he sent me a telegram a few days later telling me to check it for next semester. I think it might be a good idea to wait around and try for that. I am not sure about what I will do, but at the present that seems to be the best plan.

I had my first little note of encouragement the other day and have been writing pretty steadily ever since. I sent that story "The Spotlight" to Mr. [Donald] Berwick on *The New Yorker*, and he wrote me a long letter back telling me that the story did not come off as it was, but that he thought it was potentially a good story. He said he would like for me to do some more work on it and let him see it again. I switched it around to third person, as he suggested, tried to smooth it up a little bit, and sent it back to him. It worked some better, I think, in third person, but I don't believe the story will live up to his expectations. I squeezed as much out of it as I could, but I don't have much hope for it. I am still waiting to hear from him now, and Gwendolyn turns pale every time I go for the mail. Even if he does not buy it, he at least gave me a good bit of criticism and encouragement which I appreciated. It set me to going a little bit, at least, and I wrote one pretty fair story and got a start on another one last week.

I haven't heard from Tom [Greet] lately. I owe him a letter though, and I probably won't hear until I write it. I miss the old class now that it's school-time and I haven't got anywhere to go. It would be nice to go back through that year again. I

---

* John Selby's class in novel-writing at Columbia University.

would certainly do a damn sight more work than I did. I really wasted a lot of time.

There's not much news. If by any possible chance I happen to sell that story, I'll let you know. Thanks again for everything you've done.

Sincerely yours, Mac

P.S. I hope you don't mind my typing this, but I have a hard time making my writing readable.

By the way, my sister, Mitzi, the one who is traveling around with the Barter Theatre (she's an assistant electrician, I think; understudying a girl who, so she says, looks very frail to her) will be coming through Durham sometime soon, and she has been wanting to meet you. I just wanted to warn you that she will probably try to get in touch with you if she can. Mac

About mid-November, two of his Duke contemporaries in New York, William Styron and Edgar Hatcher, put Hyman up for a week while he looked for an apartment and a job. He worked briefly as a shipping clerk in Doubleday Book Store. His wife found work as a fashion model.

To his parents, from Brooklyn, December 4, 1947.

Dear Mama & Daddy,

I wrote you all a long letter Sunday night, kept it in my pocket all day Monday to mail it, then got to thinking that I had griped too much in it about you all not writing, & didn't mail it at all. I don't intend to do much griping now, but I don't see why you can't write me a note. I have been gone three weeks now & haven't heard anything. I know one reason is that I kept writing & calling Gwendolyn, telling you to get the news through her, but I think it's foolish to hold back on that account. I had to try to get things straightened out about when Gwendolyn would come up here; I knew she would give you all all the news; and I simply haven't had the time or the patience to sit down & write exactly the same things twice.

By the way, Gwendolyn came in Wed. (yesterday) & to-night cooked supper here at the apt. You don't know what a relief it is to have somewhere to go after I get off from work. I'm really glad she is here.

The job I have is not much, but it is hard work. The other day I had time out only once to sit down & smoke a cigarette. They are paying me, as you know, only $33 a week & I am having to put out 18 of that a week for the apt. Obviously, that doesn't leave much. I think maybe I can get a better job after Xmas, though, & we can get along a little better. My job now is a sort of glorified stock boy. I have to check charge accounts, mail out books, write up copies of C.O.D., insurance, etc. The people have been nice to me & seem to think I'm a good worker, but I'm already beginning to get a little tired of it. I suppose I'll get used to that, though.

You don't know what I would give to be at home now. If I ever get my foot in the door of a publishing house & get where I know I can do something with writing—or when I find out I can't—I'll be on my way back pretty fast. I couldn't imagine a more idealistic life than making my living writing & living around home. Maybe if I can ever get started I can do that, but of course, it sounds too good to be true. I am really going to miss being there Xmas. I wish we could have worked it out so we could be there—I wish we had had the money to make the trip, but we can't now. Every once in awhile now I get to thinking I would be perfectly satisfied to come back to Cordele, get a job at a filling station & live out on the river the rest of my life. I would like to be able to do that, but still I know I will never be satisfied unless I am writing or trying to write—and there's a kind of misery in that, too. There doesn't seem to be any way out other than by trying it. . . .

Love, Boy

To William Blackburn, from Brooklyn, December 14, 1947.

Dear Dr. Blackburn,

 . . . I stayed with Styron & Hatcher * for about the first week; they were both very helpful, showing me how to get around & where to go. I started out job-hunting on the Monday after I got here. I saw Whit Burnett [editor of *Story* magazine] who talked to me for a good while but could not advise anything in the way of a job. From there I went to see Pyke Johnson.† He had just heard from you & he was damned nice to me, told me how to go about getting the apartment which I was lucky enough to find & pay a week's rent on that afternoon. I felt fine over the apartment—I had been told so many times that it was an almost [hopeless?] situation that I was surprised that I was able to get one so easily. I doubt if I would have one by now if Mr. Johnson had not suggested the way I should go about it.

Well, by that time my money was getting pretty low and after seeing Donald Berwick on the *New Yorker,* and several others, even a man on *Collier's,* I was desperate enough to take this excuse for a job that I have now. I'm glad the job will be over Xmas, though, as I have not felt much like writing at nights after I got off from work. Gwendolyn came up about a week ago and is trying to get work as a model. They have already taken a few pictures of her & there seems to be some chance in her doing all right with it.

Got off from work early the other night to sit in on Hiram Haydn's class.‡ Styron had a story in [it] which I thought was

* After a career in advertising in New York, Edgar A. Hatcher III, Duke '47, now lives in San Francisco.

† Then with Farrar, Straus & Company, now editor-in-chief, Doubleday Anchor Books.

‡ Beginning in the fall of 1947 and continuing for thirteen years, Hiram Haydn—scholar, editor, novelist, teacher—taught a class in novel-writing at the New School for Social Research. He was editor-in-chief at Crown Publishers, then became New York editor for Bobbs-Merrill, then rose to be editor-in-chief at Random House. He was also one of the founders of Atheneum Publishers and is now a co-publisher at Harcourt, Brace & World.

very good. We went over to drink beer with him last night & he was re-working it, trying to make it a little smoother by cutting the flashback, and from what he tells me he intends to do, I think it might be better. It's good to see him trying to do something again. It looks as if it even makes him feel better.

Hatcher is still answering newspaper advertisements, trying to get a job. He is writing too, of course, but I don't think he has had any better luck with it so far than any [of] the rest of us. By the way, Styron is going to send my "Dove Shoot" to Brice * to see if he can't get it published in the *Southwest Review.* I hope it has some chance. I am more or less giving up the idea of ever selling it. If I could just get it published, that would help. . . .

Sincerely yours, Mac

To his parents, from Brooklyn, December 30, 1947.

Dear Mama and Daddy,

. . . This morning I got in a check from the gov.—the 20 dollars—and also about twelve dollars for the bonus I was looking for from working. I've had a hard time cashing checks —the Holts [Gwendolyn's parents] sent us one too—and have had to go to about five different banks trying. I finally was about to give up and Styron said he would carry them up to his bank with me, endorse them, and they would cash them. So yesterday I did that—also cashing the bond—and now we have something over two hundred and fifty dollars, so I feel we will be getting along all right for awhile. Of course, I'll also have the twenty a week coming in from the gov. until I get a job, and that can pay the rent.

I'm pretty proud of Gwendolyn. I know you haven't heard it yet, but the other day, they took her on as a Power's Model

* Ashbel G. Brice, then editor, now director, of the Duke University Press.

without giving her a course or anything, and it seems they expect her to do all right. She's happy about it, and I'm happy for her as that's what she wanted to do, and it will not take up so much of her time as a regular job would. . . . Since then she has been getting up composites and is out today taking them around to the different studios, and is pretty happy about the whole thing. By the way, they told her she could ask for *only* five dollars an hour now because she was a beginner, but could go up to ten in a little while. She seems to have done all right and I think she has been mighty lucky to get what she wants with the ease she did.

I'm not just sitting around myself even though it might seem so. This morning I had to go see the Vets. Administration again, and tomorrow will have to go see the employment bureau about a job. I have been doing some writing too and for once I am moving along on what seems to be a pretty good start in a novel at last. I got "The Spotlight" back again, though. Donald Berwick has left the *New Yorker* and some other fellow read it and wrote back to me. I'm through with that story for awhile anyhow.

But I do want to tell you what I'm trying to do in the novel.* As you know, I have made one false start after another for months now, only having a vague idea of what was going on. Since I got up here I have written the first chapter of the last idea I had about five times, each time from a different point of view, and never really getting anywhere except learning from my mistakes. I was really on the verge of just giving the idea up when Saturday night, it seemed that the thing just suddenly came clear to me as a whole, not only from viewpoint and characterization and style and attitude, and so on, but even the construction of it. So Sunday I started typing, and I sat at this damn typewriter that day for eight hours and got to bed at about two-thirty the next morning, worked on it again yesterday, and got Styron to look over what I had done.

* First mentioned in the letter of June 23, 1947, above.

He had read all the other attempts I have made and seems to think that this one is moving along all right, much better than anything else I've done, and I think so myself. I honest to God think I might even be able to finish it. And at the rate I've been going, I don't think it would take many months to do it in. I have kind of gotten exited [excited] about it this time —I guess that's obvious, though—and I feel this is the best chance I have ever had to do one. It stays on my mind a good bit of the time now and I don't go to sleep too easily, but it doesn't bother me as long as I think I'm doing something. I know I shouldn't build all this up, though, as I know you will be disappointed if it does not work out, but I really think I have the feel of it this time. I hope so, anyhow. The thing that I am so pleased over is that it seemed to develope just naturally as most of my short stories have. Most of the short stories I do that are successful at all are those that I have thought about and tried over and over, never quite seeing them clearly, until one day much later, the whole thing just becomes clear and natural. This idea has worked out in very much the same way. I have been fooling around with it, as you know, for about four months now, and it is not until now that I think I can see the whole thing. At least, I think I can see it. I hope I can.

I don't know what kind of job I will get yet. If I can keep going on this thing as I am now, I don't want to take a chance of getting a full-time job and maybe slacking off on it. We are getting along all right now on the money we have, and I believe that the best thing for me to do is to get a part time job that might at least pay the rent until I see what I am doing with this. Gwendolyn insists that I don't get a full-time job right now because she feels with her job, and with the money I am getting from the gov., or with what I will get from a part time job, we'll be able to get along all right. I think so too. If the novel does not seem to work, I'll go ahead probably and get a full time job and go back to short stories again, but right now, I know that the best thing for me to do is to get as much done on this as I can. Anyhow, we can hold out for a month or two on what we are getting now.

I know you must be tired of hearing me rave on about finances, but I'm beginning to see they play a pretty important role in living. I'll try to write a better letter next time as I know you can't get much out of this one. Tell Bobbie Lee [the Hymans' cook] and everybody hello, and let me hear from you.

Love, Boy

To his parents, from Brooklyn, mid-January, 1948.

Dear Mama and Daddy,

Just got back from the Vet's Administration again and found your letter waiting here. It seems that everything on earth happens in Cordele. That was really bad about Iris and Cousin Kitty—I know it must keep you pretty well upset around there. Tell Bobbie Lee we're right proud of her for the way she acted.* I'll try to write to Nell and Idie sometimes soon. I know they must be taking it hard about both Cousin Jule and Kitty.†

Gwendolyn is out again today carrying around composites to the different studios and for the rest of the afternoon I'll stay here and try to write. I thought I would send you this letter to let you know what I have in mind for the next few months and to let you know what the Prof. [Hiram Haydn] thinks, as you asked me.

I still don't have a job but am not too worried over it as I am getting the twenty a week from the gov., which is about as

* Bobby Lee tried in vain to rescue Iris Cox, the daughter of one of the Hymans' neighbors, from burning to death.
† Cousins Jule and Kitty Forrester had recently died.

much as a part-time job is going to pay me anyhow. I was offered one part-time job in the afternoons teaching basket ball, but I didn't take it because I don't know enough about it. That's one sport I never could do much with. I ought to be getting one in the next few weeks, though, if I can find one somewhere. We're both convinced that it will be best for me to do that so I can have plenty of time to write on the side.

Last week I wrote something like thirteen thousand words on the start I have, then hit a kind of snag and started back at the first again from another approach and have about two thousand words done that way. I can use nearly all the other material along with it, though, so I haven't wasted any time. It still seems to be going fairly well and if I can get the effect out of it I'm planning it might be all right.

Yesterday, I went up to see Styron and it seems that he had been up to see Hadyn [Haydn] again (he's the fellow teaching the class, and also editor of Crown Publishers) and Hadyn told Styron that next semester—that will start in a couple of weeks—he is going to have a novel course with a maximum of ten students, all who will be working on novels, and that he would pick only those he thought could turn out a novel that could be published. He said it was a kind of commercial venture on his part as they are looking for new writers, and that he could almost guarantee that those he picked would be publishing novels in not too long. He said he was going to have them meet three hours a week (from eight until eleven at night) and he was going to work hell out of anybody in it. That sounds pretty fine to me. Of course, I wouldn't be giving all the build-up over the class if I wasn't going to get in it. Styron said Hadyn asked him if he thought I would care to be in the class, and of course it sounds fine for me. I hope I can have a couple of good chapters by the time the class gets started.

I thought I told you before (you were asking what he thought of my work) that Hadyn had read three of my stories to the class. The day I went up to see him the first time I carried him three, and he told me that he might read one of them the next night if they were good enough—and he was decent enough to read all three of them. I think he likes my stuff pretty well—at least, it seems that way to me—and I know he can help me, and I know I need help. . . .

Love, Boy

To his parents, from Brooklyn, March 29, 1948.

Dear Mama and Daddy,

. . . There is not much news that Gwendolyn has not already written you. She told you, I think, that we are planning on leaving here this summer as there are not [any] classes and not much excuse to hang around, plus the fact that this apt. will probably be like the inside of a boiler room in hot weather and that neither of us particularly care for the place. For a while we traveled around on Long Island—they have small towns out there with trains running into the city—to see about an apt. if we decided to stay up the summer, but then we decided we wouldn't stay even if we could find one. For one thing, I don't know anybody and would have a pretty hard time just staying by myself all day. The fact that there won't be any classes this summer more or less clinched the matter.

As you all have told me all along, I think maybe the best thing I can do is to get a job teaching somewhere.* That will give me time off to write and also give me something to do. I just can't get along staying by myself with nothing to do all day. Kind of wears you down doing nothing. Anyhow, those

---

* During the following summer Hyman and his wife took courses in education at Georgia Southwestern College in Americus, a town about fifteen miles west of the Hyman cottage on Flint River.

are the plans we are making, even though they are pretty vague at present.

G. got her a job today and made ten dollars. Felt like celebrating but G. had to pose for two hours and is naturally worn out. She has a chance for another job tomorrow for a picture that will go on a book cover. She's supposed to be a Jewish girl in it. I think her name might swing the deal.*

By the way, we got us a puppy yesterday. We went first to some kennels where they had them for a minumum of seventy-five dollars so we were about to give it up when we found a place that had mixed breeds to get rid of. We finally got a little brown mongrel—half fox terrier and half spitz, I think —for five dollars. It's about eight weeks old, female, and looks something like a rat. G. liked it because it looked "pitiful." They wouldn't let us have her when they learned we lived in Brooklyn as it is a kind of Be-Kind-to-Animals place and they don't believe in subjecting any animal to a life in Brooklyn, but they agreed we could have him when we told them we were going back to Georgia this summer. That might sound like a joke but it's the truth.

Styron and I went up to see the man [Pyke Johnson] at Farrar Straus Pub. the other day, and he offered again to see if he couldn't get some of my short stories published. I'm working on them now a little bit. I am re-writing one and as soon as I finish it, I'll carry them up to him. I don't have much hopes on it, though. Anyhow, I guess it's worth a try.

I'm sending along a clipping of Mr. Hadyn out of the New York Times.† His novel just came out and it's on most of the book displays up here. I haven't read it yet, but the reviewers speak pretty highly of it. As you can tell from the article, he's pretty good. Don't see how he does as much as he does and

* Hyman's Jewish name belies his English, Protestant background on both sides of his family.
† Two reviews of The Time Is Noon, New York Times, March 28 and March 29, 1948.

still takes an interest in a bunch of would-be writers. He seemed right glad to have me back and seems to be interested in my work. I talked to him about it a little the other night and he suggested that I work out an outline on it so that I can have it to go on after I leave here. I'm going to see him at his office in a week or so, I guess.

By the way, Styron is leaving N.Y. too this summer.* From the way things look, it seems that he will be able to get an advance and a contract to publish his novel when he finishes it. It's good stuff, too. He'll probably be through with it before the year is out. It makes me feel right sorry for myself. Seems as if I never get anything done. . . .

Love, Boy

To his parents, from St. Augustine, Florida, September 30, 1948.

Dear Mama and Daddy,

 . . . Of course, by now you know that we are teaching and so far, I guess it is all right, even though it is pretty much of a strain on you having to listen to it all day, putting up with one class after another. We get up about seven and go pretty steady until three-thirty or four in the aft., then have to come back and plan out the lessons for the next day that night. As far as it being a job in which you get a lot of time off, it just isn't. Another thing about it is the silly restrictions we have to put up with, such as not being able to smoke (I usually just leave the campus during recess and walk away far enough so that it will be all right) and having to be on duty most of your lunch hour and things like that. I guess one of the main

---

* He was to be in Durham for a year, where he would occasionally read early sketches of what was to become *Lie Down in Darkness* to friends at the home of Ashbel Brice.

things the job demands is patience, which I don't have too much of. I answer fool questions all day long, have to read stories to them, and discuss the same stories, that are pretty lousy. I have a pretty hard time trying to encourage them to try to read stuff that isn't worth the paper it's written on. Anyhow, though, I've gotten along with it all right so far but I know now even better what I knew before I ever started it, that I'll never consider making a career out of it. I hear anyhow that bricklayers get paid a lot more and I'm sure the work is a lot easier. Of course the main trouble is discipline. I made the mistake of assuming they were all there to learn something and treated them more as human beings than students, gave them a little bit too much freedom and so on, and now it's hard to calm them down. The only class that has taken advantage of it is my home room and I'm afraid I'm going to have trouble with them. I've been able to hold my temper pretty well for the most part, except on one occasion when three boys were wrestling in the middle of the aisle when I was trying to talk. I got so mad that I practically threw one of them in his seat and then I had to walk out of the room for a few minutes before I could settle down enough to talk. They can really get on your nerves sometimes. The trouble is that we don't have any way to punish them and they know it. There is a law against whipping them and you can't keep them in because most of them ride the bus. Therefore, all we can do is threaten. I guess it will work out though.

I'm doing a little bit more writing now and am getting back in the swing of it, I think. Bought a second hand desk for 3.50 and a top for two dollars and we fixed it up so that it looks all right. I can ignore the school business as long as I can keep up the writing all right.

Got a long letter from Styron today. I had written him a short letter telling him we were down here, and so on, and I guess he answered the same day he got it. I'll send the letter to you later. It seems to me he was hinting a good bit on coming

37 ·

back to Cordele again.* He seems right pitiful sometimes. By the way, he was sick in bed when he wrote to me and from what I could get out of the letter, it seems that he is getting into about the same state I got in in New York. They had had a doctor out to see him so I guess this time it was a little more than his imagination. I know he would appreciate getting a letter from you as he thought so much of all of you so I'm sending along his address in hopes that you will write him at least a short note. The address is: Bill Styron, 901—Fifth St. Durham, N.C. . . .

Love, Boy

Hyman taught school in St. Augustine for one semester; his wife, the full year. In February, 1949, he drove a laundry truck for a week. Then for about four months, he sold ice cream at a stand on the beach, working at his typewriter in his spare time. By summer he had completed a first draft of Take Now Thy Son.

To his Grandmother Nell, from St. Augustine, March, 1949.

Dear Nell,

I hope by the time you get this that you're up doing a jig again. But if the doctor dismisses you this time telling you he wishes he were in as good health as you are again, the way he did one time, I remember, I'll do a jig for you myself. Gwendolyn and I decided the other night you ought to come down here to recuperate when you get up and about. You think you and Idie could make it? It would be a good trip for both of you and give G. a chance to explain her symptoms to somebody. I know them all so I think she gets rather tired of telling them to me. Every time she gets hungry, she decides she is "crav-

---

* He had visited the Hymans on Flint River for a fortnight in the early summer.

ing" and she walks around with her hands over her stomach as if she's afraid I'm going to kick it or something. I think she's the most pregnant person I've ever seen.

Still getting along all right on my job and like it fine, especially on rainy days when there is nobody at the beach. I spend most of my time at work reading and only get up when somebody pokes his face over the counter and coughs once or twice and asks me kindly for an ice cream. The rest of the time is pretty much my own and just so long as the weather stays miserable I'm happy with it. You meet some people every once in awhile, most of them tourists who all ask me the same questions so that by now I have pretty much stock answers for them—how far you can drive down the beach, how cold the water is, what is the price of avocadoes in January, and so on. You meet some peculiar people too, so much so in fact that you might think you were in a zoo or maybe in Leesburg. Today a woman dangled her head over the counter and wanted to know if I had ice cream. Now right above the stand in letters about a foot and a half high on both sides, and all over the stand in red and black, are signs that say ICE CREAM, but I told her Yes anyhow as politely as I could and started to get out a cone. But then she wanted to know where the ice cream came from. From Palatka, I told her. "Whose ice cream is it?" "Carlin's," I said. "What kinds?" "Butterscotch and vanilla." "Do you have the Dixie Sticks or popsickles?" "No'm, just butterscotch and vanilla." Then she wanted to know what kinds of cones we had and I went over to the can and got one out, held it up for her to examine, and she finally said, "Yes, I like that kind," which, I suppose, was to make me jump for joy, but didn't, and I said, "Butterscotch or vanilla?" "Does the butterscotch have nuts in it?" "Not whole nuts," I said. "Just little specks of them. But I wouldn't swear that they were nuts at all" "How's that?" "Butterscotch and vanilla," I said. "Well," and then she had to stop and think and she twisted her face around and weighed it this way and that and finally came out with her face brightening up, saying, "Give me one dip of each. How much are the cones?" "Ten cents," I said. "One dime." "All right," she said. "I'll take one," and by that time I would have gladly bought her one and ground nuts up for it too just to get rid of her. But I finally prepared it and smoothed it up for her so that she wouldn't have to bite off any rough edges and wrapped a napkin around it and handed it to her and watched her unroll a tongue about the length of a hound dog's and lick at it and then say to me, "You know, I've had a cold for a week and just can't taste a thing." But you have to make a living, I guess. I'm afraid you do. . . .

Love, Boy

P.S. This is for Idie, too, of course. I'm just addressing it to you because you are the invalid this month.

To William Blackburn, from Macon, Georgia, August 10, 1949.

Dear Dr. Blackburn,

Things have been in such a stir since I have come back down here that I have not up until now felt that I had time to write.* Gwendolyn was all right when I got in here Saturday night but they did not know when the baby might come— could be any minute or in two months, they said. So I got a room up here and spent most of my time out at the hospital waiting around until the next Saturday when the doctor decided we might as well take her back home and let her wait it out there. It seems he thought it would be about a month, at

---

* The Hymans returned from St. Augustine to their cottage on Flint River about July 1, and then Hyman spent about three weeks in Durham revising his novel.

least, but that she would have to stay in bed for that time. Anyhow, we carried her home Saturday (65 miles) and she was all right up until that night when she went into labor and had to come back again. Put her in the back of the car again and trying to get her up here in time, had to drive between 75 & 80, getting stopped by the police one time & followed by them another, but got up here around three o'clock Sunday morning. The baby, a girl, was born about five, put immediately in the incubator with oxygen (it was about two months premature) and at first did not seem to be able to make it. Now, though, it is doing much better and the doctor is encouraging in his attitude. The baby will probably have to be here about a month. . . .

They brought your letters to me from home and you don't know what they have meant to me. I know there is still lots wrong with the story—in fact, I had decided the thing was hopeless, but since hearing from you that you think it does have potential possibilities, I feel so much better about it that I even want to go to work on it again. It had come to the point that I even dreaded looking at it. The funny thing is that I was aware of most of the things that you said were wrong, but had not even considered any of the things you said were right. In fact, as far as I was concerned, up until you wrote to me, the whole thing was just as terrible as such things as "He did not say anything" which I had noticed before and was disgusted with. Anyhow, I want to try it again and I thank you. Thank you, too, for the "bill of particulars" of the things you liked. I'm beginning to believe that I thrive much better on praise than I do criticism. But God knows it is hard to work when it all seems hopeless. It's not any fun that way.

Don't know just what I'm going to do now. I'm not sure that the job I mentioned to you (traveling for the Vet's administration) is going to come through. Will probably stay [in] Cordele for awhile. Have finally decided that I'm going to have to find something outside of writing to try to make a living with. Then I can write what I want to and when I want to without being pushed by any outside considerations. It's the only way I can see. If I try to depend on the writing to live, then the writing is going to be pretty bad and I don't care about doing it if it's going to be that way. I had just as soon do something else for a living. Then maybe I can write and enjoy it. I don't like that business of feeling I have to write to live. Takes all the pleasure out of it.

So much for me and my plans. It's easy to see where my mind dwells. Had a letter from Styron the other day but have not had a chance to answer it yet. He still seems to be doing all right. Give everybody my regards. Will write to Brice today or tomorrow.

Sincerely, Mac

p.s. You should have seen Gwendolyn beam when she read your letters. Better for her than a tonic. She thanks you, too, for all the trouble you've taken & all the help you've been.

p.p.s. Just started "Precious Bane" and like it. My Sister had just finished it, said she enjoyed reading it as much as any book she's read. The woman [Mary Webb] can write, all right.

The birth of his first child dramatized for Hyman the fact that he needed money. He was without a job and his savings from the war years were exhausted. In November, therefore, he reenlisted in the Air Force, taking his family out to Mather Field, near Sacramento, California, on borrowed money. Here he prepared himself as an instructor in navigation. During the Christmas vacation, he again revised his novel, renting a room in the Bachelor Officers' Quarters in which to work.

To his parents, from Mather Field, December 20, 1949.

Dear Mama & Daddy,
 . . . I wish youall could see her [his daughter Gwyn] now.
I'm just beginning to be sorry you won't be able to see her
grow up. She's as healthy as you could ask and plenty strong
—and seems to be much happier than she used to be. She
laughs all the time now—sometimes out loud—especially
when Gwendolyn says something to her. And in the last few
days, she has found her voice a little bit and tries to talk back.
Sometimes she makes sounds louder than she expected & it
scares her, but she really is trying to talk now. G. is feeding
her pablum & egg yolks now and she eats like a glutton. Start
her on bananas in a week or so. I don't think she has slept in
her own bed more than twice since we've been here. G. can
always find some excuse to have her with us. . . .
Love, Boy

*At mid-winter, Hyman's anxiety over flying had caused him to
be hospitalized with ulcers for a month. Within a fortnight
after writing this letter, he was granted a leave before report-
ing to Ellington Air Force Base near Houston, Texas. In the
meantime he had finished* Take Now Thy Son, *on which he
had worked intermittently for two and a half years, and had
sent it to a publisher in New York. Thanks to the encouragement of his wife, he had begun writing sketches for* The Recruit, *the story of Will Stockdale, eventually to be called* No
Time for Sergeants.

To his parents, from Mather Field, March 29, 1950.

Dear Mama and Daddy,
 . . . I've written twenty thousand words in the last week
—that plus the part I did in the hospital gives me something

like forty thousand words on this one which means that it is about half finished. Dont work here at the house anymore unless I can help it—just brought the typewriter home to-night to get this off. It makes things a lot better too as I'm not worried about working all the time I am home and we can use the nights for doing something we want to do instead of me getting in here to type. Have been going out to the field on Sundays for about three or four hours anyhow just to keep it going as I have learned its not a good idea to stop one and try to take your time when it's moving all right, as this one is. I like it much better than anything I have done for awhile and feel sure that if it does not collapse somewhere along the line I ought to make a pretty good one out of it. I guess writing fast is the best way I can do it. That business of sitting down and trying to plan out something and then working on it steadily just doesnt seem to work. By the way, I got a letter from Bob Loomis a week or so back wanting to see the other novel (he's a reader for a publishing house) * but there are some changes in it I want to make before I send it out again and I dont have time to do that now. Also got a letter from Styron. He has finished his novel and it will come out later this summer,† is being called back into the Marines, where he says he will recuperate after the grind. . . .

By the way, I'm pretty sure I'm going off of flying status for good. I didnt have to request it—they said they could ground me on the ulcers without my putting in a request, so they have sent that off. I still dont have the orders on it, but they havent yet rescinded the orders taking me off in the first place when I went to the hospital. So it should work out all right and it really makes things a lot better. Now I can at least set up a kind of routine and get some work of my own done and not have to stop it for days at a time until I've lost interest in it. I

* Robert D. Loomis, Duke '49, was at this time a reader for Denhard, Pfeiffer, & Wells. After working for Appleton-Century-Crofts, then for Rinehart & Company, Loomis became an editor at Random House in 1957. The "other novel" is *Take Now Thy Son.*

† *Lie Down in Darkness* was published by Bobbs-Merrill in August, 1951.

guess in time I will have to get me another specialty because I probably wont be around here long off flying status as an instructor. Think I'll try out for intelligence or something—believe I would like that. There's still a chance of a promotion —I understand that I will be put in for it, but I dont know now whether it will come through or not, being off flying status. Wish it would as it would certainly add some money and I'd like to have it anyhow. . . .

Took the baby to the zoo this afternoon after I got back from the field. The couple across from us went along too—in fact I think they wanted to take her by themselves. She's getting along better now—she's stopped a lot of the whining she was doing, and she plays outside a good bit of the day. Already she has a suntan that looks months old. The other day she tore into a little boy that lives near here—he's four years old—and had him crying and calling his mama before G. could get us outside to stop her. G. watches her pretty closely when she goes out, but it seems she's learning to take care of herself. . . .

Love, Boy

To William Blackburn, from Mather Field, April 8, 1950.

Dear Dr. Blackburn,

. . . I have started playing around with another one which seems a little better so far. It's just playing, though. If nothing comes of it, it won't bother me. But so far it does seem like a good idea, even though I'm just letting it go the way it wants to, and it is still holding up. I guess writing is a habit just like anything else. I had promised myself not to bother with it for awhile after I got through with this one. But when I let it go a few days, I start getting the old miseries and it's the best way I know to get rid of them.

Don't know about the army anymore. I might try to get out

after I get down to Ellington. I'm getting pretty tired of navigation, radar, Loran,* and all the rest of it. It looks as if six months is the limit on any job with me. Takes me just about that length of time before I'm quite sure I'd rather do something else. I have thought about going through pilot school but I don't know. At least, it will be a change from navigation and I feel sure that I would like that better than navigating. Anyhow, it would be a change for awhile. If I decided to get out and can't, I'll probably do that. Will probably be back in again when the next war starts, though, so I don't guess it makes much difference. I have decided that when Truman flies pilot and Vaughn † co-pilot and [Dean] Acheson as gunner, I'm going to be along to navigate them. But up until then and up until the war, I don't feel very cooperative.

Thanks for sending along the clipping. I'm glad to hear about the prospects you've got now. Hope some of them do some good work for you. Just finished *The Young Lions* which is quite a book. That and *The Naked and the Dead* are enough to make anybody feel humble. Those boys [Irwin Shaw and Norman Mailer] can really write. . . .

Mac

To William Blackburn, from Houston, June 30, 1950.

Dear Dr. Blackburn,

. . . I wanted to tell you about the novel [*Take Now Thy Son*]. Mr. Hadyn ‡ read it soon after I mailed [it] to him and wrote me back a letter that did my ego a lot of good and made Gwendolyn mighty happy, but said they would have to turn it down. It was such an encouraging rejection, though, that it

---

* Loran: Long Range Navigation, a system by which an aircraft can determine its position by radar and radio signals sent from known stations.

† General Harry H. Vaughan was military aide to President Truman.

‡ Haydn was then editor-in-chief at Crown Publishers.

did make me feel better about everything—nicest turn-down I've ever had. Anyhow, he said he thought it was publishable and said he was going to send it to a few places himself to see if he could do some good with it. First, he sent it to a friend of his at Scribner's. Just heard from that the other day—another rejection but again a fairly good comment. Anyhow, he is going to try a few other places before sending it back. If I hear any good news about it, I'll let you know. I've been hoping to be able to let you know about it this time, but I guess I was expecting too much. Actually, though, not being able to publish has become such a usual state that I'm so used to it, it doesn't bother me much anymore. I guess someday I might be able to reach the point where I can get along without any hope of it at all, for publishing or living by it or anything, and then maybe I can write with more ease, taking my time & doing at least a decent job of it, and not let it bother me any more. I guess that's the only way to beat it. Certainly, writing is not a monster exactly but it does seem to take everything it can & give nothing in return. But I guess I would get tired of hunting or swimming or anything else if I had to do it, if I made work out of it. . . .

Mac

P.S. What do you think about the war situation? They tell us around here to keep the "kits packed & the muskets oiled." Actually, though, I don't think they know anymore than anybody else. The extent of the panic so far seems to have gone no further than building a fence around the Radar Lab.

M.

To William Blackburn, from Houston, November 12, 1950.

Dear Dr. Blackburn,

    I've put off writing for quite awhile as I have had a far-fetched illusion that sooner or later I could write & mention nonchalantly that my novel had been accepted by such & such. Have finally become resigned to the fact, though, that it's not going to be, as you probably already have heard. Styron wrote me about your being in N.Y. so you might know about it already. Anyhow, I heard from Mr. Hadyn the other day saying the agent wouldn't take it & that he will send it along later. Of course, there are still those places that you suggested & I'll probably send it to them, but certainly the prospect of anybody accepting it does not seem too bright right now.

Have done very little lately as I havent had the time and the inclination at the same moment. It's hard to get on any kind of schedule during the work I am doing because once I get in the habit, I have to break it to fly a few night missions. Then it's a matter of starting all over again. Have been thinking about applying for a ground job so as to get back on some kind of routine again. I have one half-way decent idea that I would like to work with, but don't know what will come of it. Doesn't seem to get much better. At present, I have about 20,000 words on it but I'm afraid most of them should be thrown out. It's supposed to be funny but at times it's just corny. It's something to do, though.

Wish I could have been in N.Y. when you were there. You all must have had a big time. Made me right homesick when Styron wrote about it.

Went out to ——— to sit in on a writing class a couple of weeks ago, but it was pretty dull.* Was kind of hoping to meet somebody who was interested in writing—just somebody to look over my stuff & let me look over his—but it seemed more of a college credit course than anything else. I have finally come to the conclusion that it's naturally harder to write by yourself with nobody to read it but yourself, than it is to have somebody interested in it. Of course, that's

* A chance remark in this course, however, led to his writing "The Hundredth Centennial." See letter of September 25, 1960, below.

obvious but I know it better every day. It's like trying to preach with no congregation, I guess. Or it's like having an argument with yourself, and the bad thing about that is that the things I know, I don't have to convince myself of and as long as there is nobody else to convince or tell, it's kind of silly to argue. Which is just another way of saying, I guess, that it would be mighty nice to be back in Durham again, in the class where somebody was bound to be listening because that's what they are there for.

Give our regards to Tom [Greet] & Brice & the others. The baby is fine & we're both getting about ready to have another. Hope the class is going all right. What about the girl from Georgia? Is she holding up?

Mac

It was not until his final year in the Air Force that Hyman gave up navigation. Then for a few months he had a desk job, working with parents and families of men who had been killed in the wars. In August, 1951, Gwendolyn Hyman became ill and returned with Gwyn to Cordele, where she awaited the birth of their second child, Katrena.

To his wife, from Houston, January 11, 1952.

Dear Honey,

. . . I now have about seven different approaches to the novel [*No Time for Sergeants*]—each one of them completely different. I think one night I have it, write furiously over the first chapter of four thousand words, and find out the next day it wasnt what I wanted to do at all. If you tell it one way, you've got to leave out this; if you tell it another, you've got to leave out something else. You remember how it first started, as a comedy told in first person from the standpoint of Will. This was to be a complete farce with nothing serious in it.

Then it seemed it couldnt be handled that way because of the different points of view and I changed it around, you might remember, and made Will confused with the world, wondering, cant figure things out. This wasnt what I wanted either. It seemed too much like wild screaming and didnt have any feeling to it. Besides, if I told it that way, many of the episodes that I had already written would have to be thrown out for they would not be believable anymore, whereas they might be accepted in the farce. So to remedy this, I created another character, Bart, who can be quite ignorant and do the episodes I already have written, and decided to make Will into a kind of naive but excitable person, who sees everything in fast movement and rushes, kind of unfeeling but loyal, but by doing this, I destroyed the new idea of having him go over to Bart's way of thinking in the end, as he was then the type of person who would not be moved—who was wildly confused and could not get attached to anyone. Also, Bart, the character I made, could not finally be taken in by Ben and at the same time have the malice that he has when he refuses to be drafted in the first place. He developed into a wild, clever sophisticated back woods character who would hardly be taken in by anyone. He had lots of feeling, tragic out-look, belligerent, joking, wildly laughing, hard drinking, and so on —none of the traits of character which he should have to do the things I had already written for him to do. It took me awhile to find this out. In fact, I had written nearly thirty thousand words before it stopped me.

So I went back and created another character, Leslie, and started all over again. Leslie was to be ignorant; Bart clever and just as he came to be; Bart taken up with the ignorant Leslie would perform the farcical episodes and finally be killed in the plane because he was taken in by Ben and wouldnt get off. At the end of this way I was going to have Bart get killed by MP's in Korea when he loses his head—he's on the verge of it all the time; he's always kind of laughing and crying at the same time and always antagonistic, joking, about South Koreans. In this way, Bart was to be conscious of the farce of the whole thing; loving Leslie the way a man does a dog and hurt and bitter by his death. At the end of it, he dies hating authority of all kind, be it Communist or American or what not.

All right, then, how does Will tell the thing? How has all this affected Will. He's the boy now—his character has changed—who can talk anybody's language, Bart's, who is smart, fast-talking; Leslie who is stupid, good natured sentimental; Ben, who is taken up by the glory of it all; he is never sure and the reason he tells it is that he is trying to find out. If that's the case, he could be several different things. And whatever he will be and however he will tell it and whatever he gets out of it, will be regulated at his level of outlook and the level of the material. Suppose then, I take level number 1, the way I had him at the first of this try, as wildly excited, making no comments, telling only what happened as if he does not know what is going on, as if he is not conscious of what is happening—just so that you see the action moving through his eyes with all the excitement that he feels (and I wrote some very good scenes this way—one of them a party before a coon hunt which really takes off) living in a world where things happen one right after the other in rapid, exaggerated, furious succession with no contemplation—with only the flashes of the scene before you. This is what I did at first, writing about ten thousand more words of it. But what will happen if it is this way? At the end when Bart is killed, and when Leslie is killed, these things are to Will as running across a road, or lightening in the sky, things that happen in this wild and furious world, and there is no feeling in him about them, if these things are to be consistent and convincing with the rest of the book. The farce is highly possible this way, but it has to be—this way—meaningful farce, but Will feels nothing and is changed in no way about them. If he were changed, the whole first part of the book seem false. And if he were not changed, if these things happen to him in a kind of consciousness which contemplated nothing, the way maybe a dog sees things, there is no reason for him to tell the story. In other words, we have episodes for the sake of episodes and they are not convincing this way.

Then suppose we give Will some feelings, enough contemplation so that he will at least have a reason for telling the story. All right, then he is quieter; he thinks and looks and wonders; he regards the world from some standpoint and this standpoint has been tampered with somehow and he wants to tell the world about it. Being this way, and in contrast to Leslie and Bart and Ben and so on, let's put him at level number two, which is as best as I can describe it, rather sad, tender, philosophical, lost in the world and not understanding it, wanting to do right and not knowing how, caring deeply about things so that in the end he is rather numbed by all that has happened. Then what do we have. A lot of feeling, more than you could get any other way (Hemingway got it in Farewell to Arms) seeing the world through hurt eyes, a slow meticulous pace in a voice that is weak and numbed. How does this sound? Fine, except for the fact that if he is that way and intends to tell the story that way—all the episodes of the farce that are convincing in the farce are completely unbelievable now. It almost makes you cringe to think about it. I wrote nearly five thousand words this way before I knew it.

Then suppose we make Will a little tougher. After all he has been through, after what he has seen and after hearing what Bart has to say about things, and giving him a reason for the story, what will that reason be? That he is sick and tired of the way things are, mad and angry, to hell with everybody, there's no good in anything the way things are. O.K. there might be a basis for that—there is one—but what about Ben and Leslie? Would somebody like that even bother with Ben or be concerned with such a story as that. He would skip all that part. He would also skip all the part in the classification, and practically every other episode that had its merits in exaggeration would have to be tempered down to logic, or otherwise it would seem like a very silly book indeed—him in all his bitterness telling things that nobody would be convinced of. It doesnt work.

Ok, there must be a way so let's take level number three where Will is nobody's fool, but clever, and sees the world in a set way, and that way is a humorous, Mark Twain kind of way, so that he can describe all kinds of exaggerations in a calm voice without even blinking his eyes, and shows you how foolish the whole thing is. He likes people fine, Leslie and Ben and Bart, but he has confidence that some things amount to something and some things dont, and it was silly of Bart to be taken in the way he was by the world, and silly for Leslie to be taken in by Ben, and so on. This is all right, maybe, because this way I can get the farce in all right that I have written— but now I have to throw out all the sections about the coon hunt and the party—and Bart cannot be a believable person that you feel for, and neither can Leslie, they have to be kind of charactatures which is all right in itself, because this is the way Will sees it, and Will can say how sorry he is about things, but you dont really feel it. He is too much at home in the world to let anything bother him much. I have a few thousand words this way too, so I know how it is.

That's part of it anyhow. Of course, basically, it comes down to the fact that I dont know what I want to say, and the reason for that is that I dont know what there is to say. Of course you dont have to know what the world is all about to do something but you have to *think* you know. And I know I dont. If it's a farce, let's write it farce and have no to-do about it. If things are rotten in Denmark, let's forget the farce and raise hell about it. If God has just pulled a dirty trick on us then let's show it that way, and make the best of what we've got. If there is any sense to killing in war or any place, let's admit it and cut out the rebelliousness. If courage is noble, let's extol it; if it's lack of common sense, let's make fun of it. If war is fun, let's say so; if it's not, let's show it that it isnt. If pleasure is foremost, let's hold up the banner for it and dont feel for anybody, Bart or Ben or Leslie or Will; if love is foremost, let's feel for everyone, which includes the South and the North Korean.

You see, honey, this is just part of it; and it's the reason I cant finish one of these things now. I dont know anything anymore. I can write and just ask questions like that easily, but I dont want to do that. There's nothing to that. I used to feel like I knew things and had a lot to say, but I dont anymore. That's the reason I cant finish anything; that's the trouble with the other book. I didnt know whether Truitt was a fool, a martyr, just ignorant, and religious man in the hands of God, a man with lots of courage (if courage is admirable) a man with a lot of love, or what. I dont know those things, and I therefore dont have anything to say. I dont trust my outlook anymore the way I used to and so everything I say is subject to question, especially by myself. I used to not look at anybody else's viewpoint for I was sure of myself, but now I do, and now it is a terrible habit with me that has such a grip on me that I question myself all the time.

. . . maybe someday we will get siturated somewhere where we are both happy and I can look up and down inside of me and not find any doubts there, and have somebody around that I think I can tell something to and they'll be interested, and maybe I can write again then. To do that, I have to live so that I dont have to think, so that there are always things around that I had rather do than bother to think, and where there is enough intellectual life around so that I will naturally be driven from it, and not take it too seriously anymore. That's asking a lot but I know it's true. . . . Hope all this has not bored you. Write soon. Love to you and the babies.

Mac

Dear Honey,

    . . . Cant wait to see you, honey. Will have everything set by the time you get here. You might think I was kidding when I said I would be glad to help with formulas and listen to babies yell, but I wasnt. It will be like a vacation almost. To think of having somebody to sit down and talk with and not think you are imposing is a lot in itself. I feel so damn useless like this anyhow, nothing to do and feeling like I'm no good for anybody. Actually, I think I might could become a pretty good home-body anyhow, if I could be doing some good writing while I was at it. The only time I ever get upset with it is when it keeps me away from doing what I think I ought to be doing. Basically, that is all that is the matter with me anyhow, I think. I dont know why it is, honey, but nearly all my life since, that is, I've been thinking about writing, anything that helped me to do that, I liked; and anything that stood in my way of that, I disliked. I told you one time, I dont know whether you remember or not, that I used to have the feeling that nothing was worth doing unless I could write about it, or if it helped me to do it. It's still the truth, I guess, even if I do forget it sometimes. But basically it's all still there, I guess, and when anybody stands in my way, or anything, I just automatically start fighting them. I think that if running a laundry truck all day was conducive to writing, that I would enjoy doing it. And anytime anything keeps me from it, when people try to get me to take jobs that will keep me from it, or worry me with other problems to take my mind off of it, or insist that I owe this or that and that certain things are my primary duty, or try to make me do things I dont believe, or act the way I dont feel, or say things that I dont mean, or make me see the other person's viewpoint, which is completely unnatural to me, to keep from hurting people and to make things more comfortable and so on, my whole insides

55 ·

all the way down to my toes rebel to such an extent that even though I try to do what seems to be right, for I know I am pretty inconsistent and that I cant justify myself sometimes, I cant do anything but hate everything that is around me, especially myself. God knows, it is hard on people sometimes being that way, but there is nothing that can be done about it. That is the way most people are really, I think, the only thing is most people are doing what they want anyhow. It's like they say about leading a horse to water. Well, they could keep me in the Air Force for the rest of my life if they could keep appealing to my sense of duty, but nobody on earth, including myself, could ever make me like it if I didnt naturally. It's the same way with so many other things, the same way with us and the family. I tried to make myself like teaching by telling myself that it was important and so on, but I was beaten at that before I started. I was kidding myself. I disliked it naturally, and by telling myself it was a duty and a necessity even made it worse. I finally came to despise it. It is not natural for a person to try to see other people's points of view all the time. It's one of the most unnatural things he can do; it can ruin him and undermine him quicker than anything. It's perfectly right and perfectly natural that each person should have his own point of view, and have pride in himself enough so that he doesnt mind disagreement, but welcomes it. You say sometimes that you cant understand why I always have to have arguments around me. I'll tell you why very plainly. Because where there is a different view-point around, an honest one, not a mean one, a person in his pride will hold up his own and believe in it, and is not faced with the necessity of trying to see the other person's side of things. A difference of opinion clears the air and livens things up and brings out the best in a person, as any fight will. It makes him into a better person because it makes him into a natural person as he then sees only his side of things, and he can center on that and use all his energies in proving it, and there is nothing on earth more satisfying than to use all your energies on something you believe in. Yes, I love to argue and fight sometimes because I always respect myself more and respect the other person more. Of course, it can be carried too far, but I have never disliked a person because of an argument. The only times I feel uncomfortable with somebody I argue with is when the other person loses his pride, as I have done with you at times and you have done with me, and instead of holding up, begins to nag you with pity and a hung-head, and appeals to your sense of mercy or duty to look at the other side of the question. I guess pity is the nastiest weapon available and I always feel rotten when I use it or when anybody else does because it shows a lack of conviction, a lack of pride or something, that is not a very pretty sight to see in a person.

Well, I got off on another essay tour, it looks like. I waste better essays and ideas writing them in letters to you than a lot of people ever publish. That might sound like conceit but it's the truth. Anyhow, I hope you have studied them carefully as you are very privileged to be the first to hear them.

I cant wait to see yall. I feel like arguing right now. Enjoyed talking to you last night. God, I bet we ran up a phone bill.

By the way, I went to the show this aft. when I got through with the apt. Saw Quo Vadis and it was real colossal with the lions eating up the Christians and Robert Taylor getting converted in the end and so on, but they did have some right gruesome scenes in it that I know you would enjoy. Wish we hadnt sold the television set now. Several people asked about you today as I went around the apts—Big Red and a couple of more whose names I dont know.

What I ought to do is quit writing to you and start writing on the novel. I doubt if you half read them anyhow. Do you?

Let me hear from you when you get a chance, and let me know when you are coming. Cant wait but I probably will. I'm real happy about it, though.

Love, Mac

In February, 1953, Hyman entered Columbia University as a graduate student on the G.I. Bill. He had saved enough money from his work in the Air Force to take care of his family in Cordele, while he gave himself a last fling at writing.

To his wife, from Columbia University, early February, 1953.

Dear Hon,

. . . My room mate just came in and went out again—he's a pretty nice fellow and doesnt know anybody either, and it's somebody to talk to every once in a while. He's a former Marine, just coming to college for the first time, though he is 24, from Pa. and is already picking up my accent for some reason. In fact I think he has begun to sound more Southern than I do. The more I think of it, the less I care about getting a room to myself. I would get mighty lonesome that way and he is company, and doesn't seem to have a nerve in his body. He goes on to bed finally and I keep on typing; it doesn't bother him at all, thank God. . . .

I love you, Mac

To his wife, from Columbia University, February, 1953.

Dear Honey,

. . . New York is about the same as it was. I know I don't belong here. The night after I arrived, I started in a place to get a cup of coffee & laying on the floor with two policemen around her was a woman who had just dropped dead. They were trying to find out who she was. Everybody else was still sitting around eating. I did not hang around, though; I didnt want coffee that bad.

Didn't get anything done last night. Went through my stuff & that was about all. My room mate is talkative in a right boring way & has found a place you can get breakfast for 22¢ &

dinner for 34¢ & many other fine things. I should be more like him, I know. He has a girl that he talks about & wants some day to be some kind of executive. He's all right, though, only unusually yankeeish, plodding, & respectfully ambitious. He was damn decent about letting me borrow his pencil yesterday. I honestly felt I should offer to pay for what lead I used, but I think he enjoyed doing the favor. Anyhow, I finally went across the street & got a beer, then read for awhile. . . .

I wish to God Styron or somebody like that were around that you didnt have to arrange dates with, but were such bums you could drop in anytime & they were free. By the way, he did right well with a long short story in the first issue of *Discovery* & got a good write-up.* Have'nt read it, though.

Honey, we're ready to go eat now. Let me hear from you. Write me about what you are doing & about the chillun & Cotten. I miss you & love you, God knows.

Mac

To his wife, from Columbia University, February, 1953.

Dear Hon,

I've got my typewriter back & would be using it now only it is past eleven o'clock & my roommate is asleep. Got it back this morning late & spent all aft., about five hours trying to write, & it was all pretty terrible. I jumped from one thing to the other, from this story to that—("I'll just knock this one off & then do that one" then, "No, I think I'll work on a novel") and so on until I was in pretty much of a complete frenzy & got nothing accomplished. As usual I couldnt make up my mind about how I wanted to do anything—I'm beginning to be afraid that I never will. Indecision of that sort can ruin you sooner or later. If I could just see one thing clearly I could

---

* "The Long March," *Discovery*, No. 1 (New York, 1952), 221–83.

write, but I can't do it. I try to make up my mind that *"This is what I believe things are—this is what happened then"* but I can never convince myself. I'm beginning to be afraid I am doomed by doubts at the beginning—& there is nothing worse than fear and doubt & uncertainty. You can never write as long as you doubt yourself.

But today was the first day. Maybe I'll do better later. I will try not to write about writing as it naturally bothers me & gets me upset to think that I have not done anything with it. But I truly believe this is my last try. I can't let it ruin my life, or what there is left of it. I'll have to find something else to do. . . .

Love to you, Mac

Hyman elected three courses at Columbia: short-story writing under Helen Hull, novel-writing under John Selby, and a course in literature, Comedy and Tragedy, under Mark Van Doren.

To his wife, from Columbia University, February 24, 1953.

Dear good ole hon,

I am now drinking my second beer and feel better than I have all day naturally, and I want to talk to you and dont see you around anywhere. I just got back from the short story class in which I am absolutely so far the best writer even being prejudiced about it, and it kind of perks me up knowing that all of these characters who are so well educated and can speak in such long words cannot write as well as old me can. This Miss Hull is good too; I mean she doesnt miss anything about anything and as far as I can see, she hasnt been wrong many times, and neither does she try to make anybody feel good; she tells you just what she thinks and why and she knows why too. I think she is a very fine teacher. Doesnt care much about anybody though, only knows them through their writing, it seems, but that is one thing she knows. She is having another novel [*Landfall*] come out next week by the way; dont know whether she herself can write or not. She's a little old grey-headed woman about sixty something I guess, and I would like to take my novel to her if I could, if she would fool with it, only I dont know. I mean I would trust what she says. . . .

However I did work all day on the Will Stockdale story; got up at eight this morning and started on it and kept at it up until four when I had to go to class. Course, I ate in between times. I couldnt figure out how to work it again; whether Will is smart or dumb; whether to be laconic or exciting and so forth. I worried over it and did this and the other and prayed about it and in the absence of spiritual intervention, flipped a coin on it, and finally got off some few thousand words in the laconic style, though I dont really know about it yet.

I also this morning got three of your letters—Thurs. Friday and Sat.; I got the Thurs. one first, and when I went down again the other ones. Thank you honey. And dont say I dont read your letters because I go over them and go over them, only I forgot about the insurance. . . .

I love you, Mac

To his wife, from Columbia University, March 6, 1953.

Dear Hon,

. . . I dont know what it is, but I really feel lousy most of the time—either my chest is hurting or my heart or I have indigestion; feel like I cant eat most of the time and whenever I lay down, my heart starts palpitating until I finally have to get back up again. The only time it seems that I can lay down when it isnt is after I have had a few beers. The only other thing that bothers me at the moment is that I get so damned tired; feel like I am completely exhausted even though I have not been doing too much. I know it's nerves and all but it gets me down sometimes. That's the reason I went on to the show tonight. I had written most of the day since I got up this morning and I write too *hard* when I write or something so that after a little bit of it, I feel pretty well worn out. For the last two days I have done only two chapters and most of that was copying and changing around from old stuff that I have, and that really is not very much when you take that into consideration, plus the fact that one of the chapters is not much good and I will probably have to do it over. I had it in my mind to get about seven done before Monday night class but I guess that was too much to plan on. But it seems that I can stay at it only a little while at a time and then I have to get out, even though, God knows, it's usually worse for me outside unless I head for the park which is about a block away. I think by the time that I get away from here I will have a complete case of claustrophobia. Never could stand being inside for long at a time and I guess I am getting worse about it in my old age. Today I took out of here awhile and went to the park where I ran and trotted and walked for about thirty blocks I guess, and made me feel some better. There are lots of pigeons around and I usually pretend that I'm out in the woods and have a gun and they are either ducks or doves; I bagged about thirty today and made some beautiful shots.

Have not yet heard from the 100th Cent[ennial] * and am beginning to hope that they have decided to use it. . . .

Will let you know of course if I hear anything good. The money is still escaping me—from that check I gave Wed. morning—it was twenty five dollars—I now have only about ten left. Of course out of that I paid for those theater tickets, got cleaning done, went to the show tonight and bought food

* Apparently begun in Houston (see letters of November 12, 1950, and September 25, 1960), and finished at Columbia in February, 1953.

but it still seems just to run through my fingers. My room-mate makes me feel real guilty about it—he is the most saving person I have ever seen in my life; won't even eat meat because it costs; we have a long discussion on how much he has saved each day. Did I tell you that not long ago he found a place where you could get shirts done two cents cheaper? Well he did and asked me if I wanted anything to send along so I gave him two shirts, and it wasnt until later that I found out the place came to be a sixteen block walk—but I saved four cents on it. No kidding, next to him, Mr. Holt [Gwendolyn's father] is devil-may care with a nickle. He's all right, though, and we get along all right.

Let me hear from you, honey. I love you real good and miss you too.

Mac

To his wife, from Columbia University, March 9, 1953.

Dear Honey,

I have had a right flattering day in a sense and was looking forward to writing you about it, only right now I am so tired all of a sudden that I dont know how much of it I will write.

Did not quite finish up Part 3 of the Recruit to give to Selby tonight but at least finished the main writing of it so that I can probably smooth it up by next week. Did not write long yesterday (Sun.); went down to see Sister again and to see some couple that she knew and talked with them awhile, then went and ate with Mr. Reese again. And while I was there he gave me a damned nice overcoat that he said he didnt need or wear; Sister had already told me that he had asked her whether or not I would want it, and Sister said that he kind of wanted me to take it, so I did. It's a kind of brown tweed check and is much warmer than my other one, kind of sporty looking but not too much so. I was really glad to get it. It's the first time I've really been warm on a cold day outside yet.

Anyhow, today I wrote all day, then went over to see Selby who had finished reading the second part that I have [given] to him, and seemed to like it a good bit. We talked awhile and he is all for my finishing it, said he had a couple of people in mind to try to place it with if I didnt mind, which I damn well dont. He also wants to try to publish part of it in that New American Writing—the same thing that Bob [Loomis] tried, as I told him—but it seems that he had already talked with somebody about it and they are going to write me or get in touch with me. So that sounds right good even though I doubt if anything will come of that. Anyhow, he seems to have talked about it with a couple of other people, said he explained the idea to one fellow who told him that it sounded like a modern Don Quixote. As I have not read Don Quixote, I wouldnt know, but it sounds right good, I guess. Anyhow, he seems to be taking an interest in it, wants me to finish the whole thing before going back through and smoothing it up, and says that it does hold up all right. Said he believes in it and really thinks I might be able to do something with it. So I told him I would give him Part 3 next week if he would have time for it, and he says he will. So anyhow, it is now about three fourths written, except for the hell of starting back over and shaping the whole thing up, but that is something.

Well, anyhow I left there and went over to the class to wait in the library, and in the library one of the girls from the short story class came up and said that she had just finished my story (the Actress) and that I was just a genius, that was all, a genius. She's the same one that took my 100th Cent. to her mother and said her mother broke down and cried over it. So I told her I wasnt too much of a genius, but I didnt press the point, and then I left there and went back to the class where this other woman stopped me outside the door and said she just wanted to tell me that she liked my writing more than any she had heard and so on, for which I was right grateful but was reaching the point where I felt above it all; I then sat in class and ended up my evening with this other lady coming up and telling me that she had a son in the Army and that she had told him all about my story of the soldier, and that they had laughed over it and thought it was the best idea they had heard in a long time. By this time, of course, I was at the point where I would hardly go out of my way to even listen to the flattery—this kind of autograph hound thing you know, —but I gave her the privilege of listening, being as she was talking about my stuff; and she said one other thing that might interest you; she said, "It must be wonderful to be able to look on the bright side of things and laugh at things the way you do. It must be wonderful to have such an outlook." I thought you might enjoy that very much.

Anyhow, it is a kind of funny thing I am doing now; in the short story class, I am a very deep and serious genius, and in the novel class, I'm a little giggling devil-may-care humorist. Take your pick. Myself, I am beginning to give up on it.

But in case you take this seriously, all the flattery, let's do not for one moment forget that these things are passed around easily here, and that most of it came from frustrated writers who wouldnt be frustrated if they knew more about what they were doing, like me, and that none of it really amounts to anything much, except that I enjoy being thought good, as none of them is a publisher—so things are still hanging in the balance. Still, I do enjoy having the time to write and having somebody appreciate it. And this thing might work itself out after all. . . .

I'll stop now, honey as I am tired. I am going to drink my other beer and bask in my little bit of golory.

I love you, Mac

65·

To his wife, from Columbia University, March 10, 1953.

Dear Hon,

. . . My room-mate spent fifty-two cents for his supper tonight and we are quite happy over it. He is now writing for the fourth time a theme on Safety Driving which he has re-worked at least for two weeks. It runs a good two and a half pages and we have discussed every sentence in it everytime.

There was one thing in class tonight that I thought was right funny. One fellow had written this story about space flyers, how they beat the Chameleon men by using paint spray guns on them so they could see them—this was on some planet out of space, you know. Well, I thought it was right funny and pretty good as satire, and when in class I was asked what I thought of it, I said as much, and elaborated a great deal on his clever use of cliches for comic effect and so on, how ridiculous that the spray guns were in space travel and so on, only to find out later that the poor bastard was truly serious about it and had had a great deal of difficulty in deciding what color paint should be used. And all those funny cliches that I kept complimenting him on weren't cliches to him a bit. I was right mortified when I found out he was serious about it, but it didnt bother him I dont think. It couldnt bother him, I dont think. . . .

I love you a good bit.

Mac

To his wife, from Columbia University, March, 1953.

Dear Hon,

. . . Had a right good time around at Sigrid's the other night. I went around to Bob's and he and I drank beer, then picked up some pork chops to take them around to Sigrid's.

She and Mrs. de Lima cooked and we talked and it was kind
of fun. They are good people. Asked all about you and so on,
and remembered when we were up for supper and everything.
As I told you on the phone, Sigrid has won the same prize
that Styron did, a three thousand dollar scholarship to Rome,
and is going over this summer. She's doing right well, it seems,
with writing—they say her second book is mighty good and
she is now on her third one.* . . .

I love you, Mac

To his wife, from Columbia University, April 14, 1953.

Dear Hon,
 . . . Sorry the 100th Cent. upset you,† and can surely
understand how you feel, but for somehow or other, I have
not let it bother me a bit. And that's right strange as usually
the effect hits me a few days later and puts me down in the
dumps for quite awhile. But of course it has been a little
different for me this time as I talked with the fellow, and
know that he at least thinks they should have bought it, and
suggested that I try it other places. So there is nothing wrong
with the story, that I can see. It is just a matter of finding the
market for it, and I believe I'll do that sooner or later. I still
know it's a good story, and even though that is not the main
thing, it does at least amount to something.

* Sigrid de Lima was a contemporary of Hyman's in Hiram Haydn's class
at the New School for Social Research, where her mother, Mrs. Agnes de
Lima, was in charge of publicity. Miss de Lima won the *Prix de Rome*,
American Academy of Arts and Letters, for her first two novels—*Captain's
Beach* (1950) and *The Swift Cloud* (1952). *Carnival by the Sea* came out
in 1954. Since that time she has written two other novels.

† Hyman had probably telephoned his wife about the rejection of "The
Hundredth Centennial" by *Discovery*. However, the story later appeared in
the *Paris Review* (Fall–Winter, 1954–55), 9–35. The story was also collected
in *The Best American Short Stories, 1955*, ed. Martha Foley (Boston, 1955);
and in *Best Short Stories from the Paris Review*, intro. by William Styron
(New York, 1959).

And another thing is, I think, that I have stayed right busy and havent dwelled on it the way I used to. Got up earlier this morning and got in some work, and am mainly now thinking about what I am doing rather than past failures, which I know is a better thing. It becomes clearer to me as long as I am up here, that I am a right good writer, and will, if there is any justice whatsoever, be published sooner or later, and I really havent worried too much about it for awhile. But of course, it makes a hell of a lot of difference just knowing that there are people who are interested. . . .

I love you, Mac

To his wife, from Columbia University, April 22, 1953.

Dear Honey,

Just got back from supper and it is still light outside—this daylight saving time—so it still feels early to me. Anyhow, thought I would go ahead and write to you now and get it off in the nine o'clock mail, being as I didnt write last night. I didnt last night simply because I didnt have the time. I put in a hell of a day all day yesterday; wrote from the time I got up until four o'clock when I had to go to class, went to class until six, ate supper, then waited for Miss Hull in her office as I had been wanting to talk with her about my stuff and thought it was a good time to do it. Anyhow, I had a right long talk with her, told her about the situation on the novel (asking whether it would be better to give it to an agent or take it to the publishing house) and she was of the opinion (and she knows too—has a lot to do with Author's Guilds and things like that) that I take it to the publishing house myself first. She went on to say that I would save a lot by doing it and all like that; and that if I published it, I could get an agent anyhow. Seemed to be right interested in it too; also made me feel right good by saying that I had all kinds of talent and stuff like that and if there were any way on earth possible for me to keep on writing, not to give it up. Made me feel right good about it—said if there was anything she could do to help, she would be glad to do it; that she had been mighty interested in my work all the way through. Also said that she has never had an agent to handle her own novels—she does it herself; she says she does for short stories, though. (By the way, her book has been selected for one of these book guilds, so she's getting along right well lately, it seems.)

Anyhow, I guess she's right about it; that's what I will do. After talking to her, I went to class which lasted until 10:30; then got on that ungodly subway and rode for forty-five minutes down to Sisters place to take her Part 3, and pick up Part 2 that she has finished. She had been rehersing; this fellow was down there and we drank beer for awhile and went over what I wanted done; didnt get back here until after two last night, and right worn out too.

And today I've done a right good bit too, although I didn't get up until ten-thirty. But I turned out quite a bit of work, re-doing this last part, and am now about three-fourths through with that, and right satisfied with it too. Looks a hell of a lot better than it did before, and I have finally worked out the right ending I want, which I think will tie the whole thing up pretty neatly. Of course the sentences are rough as hell (everytime I look at the thing I start changing them around) but I should be through with it sometimes next week at the rate I'm going now. I started back over Part 1 again later on this aft. to turn it in to Van Doren and went through as much as I had time to in pencile and kept finding things to change again. It really does worry me, getting the right pace and things like that, and it's right hard to do in a book of this sort. So I changed a little bit of what she had typed up, even though I only had time to go through about thirty pages of it before class time. Anyhow, I gave it to Van Doren—he has been discussing Don Quixote for about the past two weeks now—seems to think a hell of a lot of it—and the more he talks the more amazed I am in the resemblance between many of the ideas in that and what I am writing. Whereas he wanted to be a knight and do everything according to the rules, Ben wants to be a soldier—not much difference there; and from what he says, Will seems to take the place of the one called Sanchos. Am glad I never read it or I am afraid I would worry about it. . . . am getting mighty ready to get out of this place; getting the palpitations and stuff again, though it's better than it was the other time. . . .

I love you, Mac

To his wife, from Columbia University, morning, May 6, 1953.

Dear Hon,

. . . Worked all day Monday up until time for class, then went to Van Dorens class—after it was over he wanted to see me in his office about the piece of the novel that he had read.* Wanted to know what I was going to do with it and kept at the idea of my taking it to Henry Holt and Co. Said he thought it was very good humor and quite a relief from the usual war stories, that he enjoyed it and so on and made me feel right good about it. Also said that he thought it should sell a lot and that he had told the Publishing house so—that's the main reason they were interested.

Anyhow, made me feel good, so I came back, worked some more on it trying to smooth out some kinks in the last part, then went to novel class, and after class when I usually write to you, wrote to Henry Holt instead as I told Van Doren that I would. And after that I wasnt up to another letter as I have

* Van Doren had agreed to accept the novel as a term paper in the course.

been pushing myself right hard here lately trying to get this thing over with and was feeling right shaky.

Yesterday, I put in the same kind of day from eight thirty in the morning up until seven last night but with different results somehow. I am mainly proof-reading now; finished the first half of it and was so disappointed in it that I could throw it away. I know I am pretty tired of it and all like that, but at the same time, it reads so lousy that I honest[ly] feel like throwing it away. It really gets me down somehow. The thing doesnt come to life the way I thought it did; the characters dont come through the way I see them—it really looks right sorry to me and I dont feel too good about it. Still, I'm going through with it—Hope to finish today or tomorrow and have it to Bob [Loomis] before the week is out and let them do with it what they will. And now I am kind of ashamed to take it down as I have been talking about it for awhile now and it doesnt come up to expectations at all. . . .

I love you, Mac

To his wife, from Columbia University, evening, May 6, 1953.

Dear Honey,

Today I have felt right lousy from the beer I drank last night, but have managed to survive and am now feeling right good. Worked all day and finished finally and absolutely on the novel; have it in shape enough to take in tomorrow to Bob, as per schedule. Comes out to be 130,000 words, which is right long. Would tell you some more about it but am so tired of thinking about it right now that I dont care to. It naturally looks so sorry to me that I dont see how anybody can read it right now, but I am just hoping that is the ordinary thing. I'm trying to have faith in the fact that I could probably be wrong, but I am somehow inclined to feel that this let-down feeling couldnt be natural or all novels would be thrown away before they ever got to publishing houses. . . .

Bob called again this afternoon about the novel and I told him I would bring it down tomorrow. Decided to call it *The Recruits,* plural. Have been hunting around for a kind of quote to put at the front of it—you know what I mean— something from Shakespeare or something like that—am now undecided between two. One is that line from Styrons book "He came to her on his knees, dragging at the heels" * with the idea that there might be something funny about the most serious of things. And the other, which I like better, is "This is definitely a violation of regulations" † from the comment by Gen. Mark Clark on the prisoner rebellion at the Korean prison camps. I thought to kind of sum the outlook up. You remember when he made that asinine comment? I got quite a kick out of it then, but just remembered it again tonight. What do you think? What do you think about the title too? . . .

I love you, Mac

To his wife, from Columbia University, May 12, 1953.

Dear Honey,

. . . About the only reason a person writes in the first place, I think, is some kind of desire to influence other people,

* The line refers to Milton Loftis and his wife Helen. It reads: "Who had come back to her . . . literally on his knees, dragging his heels, remorseful, in tears." See *Lie Down in Darkness.*

† As United Nations Commander, General Clark sent paratroopers to Koje Island, south coast of Korea, to block any further uprising, saying, "I do not propose to countenance for one moment further unlawful acts on the part of these prisoners of war." This statement reflects the tone though not the exact words of Hyman's quotation. The POWs had kidnapped the commandant of the camp, Brig. Gen. Francis T. Dodd and had forced Brig. Gen. Charles F. Colson to make embarrassing concessions to obtain Dodd's release. Both officers were demoted to the rank of colonel. See *New York Times,* May 18 and 24, 1952, Sec. 1, p. 1.

or to convey certain things to them, and if I dont feel like I'm getting that over, I dont feel too good. Have to change that a little bit, though. It's really no fun to influence anybody too much. If they are the type that will give in too easily, you dont want to bother with them. That's the reason I could argue religion with Jannace and psychology with Murphy—no worry of changing them. Reminds me of something that Van Doren had to say the other day on one of his wide varieties. He said a sure sign that you are in love with somebody is that you are always wanting to change them somehow, and went on to say that you would probably be disappointed if you ever did change them. Fits me to a Tee I know. He's a right smart man in many different ways, and yet he is human too. I thoroughly admire him and to clear the air, I did even before he read my writing. . . . Miss you and love you a good bit.

Mac

To his wife, from Columbia University, May 15, 1953.

Dear Honey,

. . . I know I'll be there by the time Gwyn has her recital —dont see how anything could come up that would keep me from it.

Will not talk about the book anymore until I find out something, and of course I will call you then. It's kind of futile to speculate on it with everything as indefinite as it is. I myself think that it is publishable and should also be right popular, but of course I have been wrong about that so many times in the past that it doesnt mean much. Just have to wait it out and see how it goes.

I've found out one thing by being here though. I've found out I can get ten times more done if I just quit thinking about what I'm doing and how things are going and all like that.

Havent planned for the future or done anything much like that—usually never even sent out laundry or wasted time on such things—just put my faith in the fact that if I kept on writing and didnt bother with the other things, they would just take care of themselves—or if they didnt, there wasnt enough I could do about them to warrant my worrying about them anyhow. I'm just hoping it worked out all right. It did in the sense that I finished the novel in about two and a half months, keeping myself most of that time kind of suspended away from reality or worries of any sort, and just having faith in the fact that when I came drifting out of the clouds, so to speak, that things would be better off somehow. It was right hard to do, especially in view of the fact that for the past few years I have acquired the habit of worrying and planning and wondering about everything, feeling that if I didnt do it, things would just collapse in front of me, so that I felt I had to question about every thing I did and every line I wrote. But this time I somehow disciplined myself not to think like that any longer, and when I got on Part four of the novel and was right up near the end and couldnt think of any good way that it *could* end, I didnt let that bother me to the extent that I felt I had to stop writing until I did figure it out, the way I have done many times before—instead I kept writing with a kind of confidence that it would work itself out by the time I got there; and it worked that way all right. The ending is right good, I think—it's good enough to sum up the whole book and bring it into a kind of focus—it has a tinge of seriousness but is really funnier than any of the first part, I think—in fact, I believe it is much better this way than I could ever have planned it anyhow, and really dont believe that I could have planned it from the first.

So at least I have found that out about writing. You just have to suspend yourself and not worry about where things are going or why you are doing them or anything else—you just have to have a kind of blind faith in the fact that as long as things are going all right, they will keep up like that somehow, even though you might not be able to imagine any way or method or anything that could do it for you. Of course, as I say, this takes a certain amount of discipline. It's like walking down a long dark tunnel with no promise of light at the other end with the feeling that if you just keep going long enough, the light will turn up. . . . In a way, though, that is the same way we have lived most of our lives. We had children when we couldnt afford them; we got married when I had no job or no way of making a living; we went off writing and things when I couldnt write and didnt know what I was doing—still the children arent starving and we're still married and I'm still writing. And I venture to say, being as I am venturing to say a lot anyhow, that if we had stopped and thought and planned carefully on each of those things, we would not have been married in the first place; but if we had we would certainly have had no children by now; and I would have given up writing and gotten me a job with the VA or something for the rest of my life. So being stupid has its points, I guess. Of course, we would have done better many times with a little more foresight—had lots less trouble and so on—but we would have lost a few things too, I think.

Of course, all of the above holds true mainly if this book gets published and so on. Otherwise it will still be right doubtful figureing, even though we do have some hot-shot chillun as far as I'm concerned. . . .

I love you, Mac

As an associate editor at Rinehart and Company, Robert D. Loomis was keen to have The Recruits *published by the firm. The firm decided, however, that it could offer only an option of $250 on the book. Hyman then took his typescript to Henry Holt and Company. At some point between this time and* *early June, John Selby introduced Hyman to his agent, James Oliver Brown.*

To his wife, from Columbia University, May 19, 1953.

Dear Honey,

. . . I hope I did the right thing today in taking the novel on down to Henry Holts. I know I am acting independent as hell for somebody who has never even published a short story, but I might as well try it that way for awhile. Havent done anything the other way, so maybe this will work. And for another thing, if I can keep from hanging on the fence any longer, that's what I'm going to do. Kind of hated to take it away from Bob because he was so anxious—or seemed that way—to have me go ahead and shape it up at the end (which it does need. This last fourth is practically a first draft as far as that goes.) and take the option and so on. And as a matter of fact, if they had shown any consideration or something, I think I would have left it there anyhow. But it seems that the editor couldnt talk with me until Friday about it, so I said to myself, to hell with it and him too, then. Damned if I wanted to sit around here for days waiting to talk with somebody when they could give me a free moment; and leaving things still kind of in the air too. I guess you have to publish a few books before you can tell them to go to hell but I thought I would give it a try anyhow.

Read the report that Bob wrote on it, and he played it up pretty big, it seemed to me. Was trying to get it on the fall list instead of the spring list and so on. So I appreciated that— and the fact that he offered to talk to Hadyn, who was going to spend the night up at his place tonight, if he could give it a quick reading. Also offered to call this Paul Brown [James Oliver Brown], the agent, who **is** supposed to be a pretty big dog, who, Bob says, never takes anything much that he doesnt sell,—and tell him what he thought of it, so maybe he would take it on. So I dont know. Went strolling into Henry Holts, which is a right big outfit with secretarys to the secretarys and so on, and said I wanted to see Bill Rainey, who is the editor-in-chief. So I guess the woman thought I was a personal friend or something and went running around trying to get somebody to talk with me (he was home, sick). So she finally got his secretary, who remembered who I was from the letters that he had written me, so I kind of bull-dozed her too. Said I was ready to go home and dint like the deal that Rinehart was offering and thought they might do better about it. I said I was in a big hurry and when could Mr. Rainey read it and give me some word on it. So she said she would try to get a fellow to read it that afternoon and have his idea on it by Thursday, and try to get it to Rainey right after that, if I would leave it (because I kept it clasped under my arm all this time, hesitating, you know—like there are people following me right now trying to steal it.) So I dont know what will come of it. I might be a fool for not taking the first offer, but I am getting very fed up somehow with editors. I want to get one that I like and keep writing if possible, but I am beginning to give up on that. Of course, it is early to give up yet I guess, but still sometimes I feel like saying to hell with everything and go get a job or something. But what else would I do? Obviously, I *can* write, if I can ever just get started. I dont know though. There seems to be some mysterious devision between me and those who publish and are considered, when I know—not bragging but just know—that I have as much or more range and feeling and ability as any of the rest of them. I feel this is true, but I dont know how to prove it except by writing and I cant keep this up unless I publish some. It kind of takes my confidence away when people dont just jump at what I write. That is vanity and nothing else, and I guess it will beat me in the long run; but right now I have it if nothing else and will be right bitter I guess, if other people dont usually think I am as good as I think I am.

Anyhow, there is another waiting spell now. I think I had better get to work on something or other as I cant stand just to sit around the way I have been doing. But it's hard to trust the words you put on paper when other people dont. That's the reason people like Blackburn were so important to me. They took my work seriously—not as something that is just one more—but something in itself, and I could write for them forever, and much better too.

Will stop now at the end of the page. I love you. Let me hear from you.

Mac

To his wife, from Columbia University, May 20, 1953.

Dear Honey,

. . . Right now there is a fire engine going by, screaming and ringing bells and people are hanging their heads out of the aprts. across the way watching it. It's gone now and there is nothing but silent people walking the sidewalk and the windows have closed, and all the idiots who exist across the way have closed the windows again, having had their excitement for tonight. . . .

Mac

To his sister Mitzi, from Route 3, Cordele, June 5, 1953.

Dear Sister,

Am returning the five dollars which I keep forgetting. Hope you havent needed it before now.

Am out at the river right now where I have been working for the past three days. Best place to work I have been in yet too. Have set myself up a desk and typewriter in this bottom room and I come out here in the morning, work until about six, then go in swimming and head back for town. At the present time, I'm trying to get up some of the short stories to send off to the agent to see what he can do with them. Planning on getting them off tomorrow.

Everybody here getting along fine. Dinah is about out of her mind, getting more unconscious every day. The latest thing she did was pick up the telephone to answer it and stand there for about a half a minute, forgetting to say anything. It wasnt until the person on the other end said, "I can hear you breathing," that she ever remembered what she had picked it up for. There is a big couch sitting in the hall at home—I havent found out yet what it is doing there; I asked Mama about it and she said something or other about it—said that Dinah had fallen over it two or three times and she had decided just to leave it there until Dinah finally noticed it, if she ever does.

The children are getting along all right too. Bought me a new suit that I like a lot and am going to wear it tonight to what they call Class Night.* I think Mama and Daddy are going to get Dinah some water skie's (or however you spell it) for graduation; Daddy is planning on getting a bigger boat and a large enough motor to pull it. . . .

Love, Brother

To James Oliver Brown, from Route 3, Cordele, June 5, 1953.

P.s. I had one idea for a novel that I wanted to fool with but I explained it to my wife and told her that I thought I might write you about the idea, but she said, after hearing it, "Oh, please don't do that—don't you *want* an agent?"

* Part of Dinah's graduating exercises at high school.

Dear Jim,

Got your letter the other day about the Atlantic Monthly reading The Recruits, and was mighty glad to hear it. I havent, as you warned, let my hopes get too high, but still it is good to know that there really are people in the world who care about reading a novel. Around here, I sometimes lose sight of that fact completely; it's pleasant to realize sometimes that there really are such things as publishing houses, books, etc.—not just figments of my imagination. The whole idea of writing here is of course something that must be kind of perverse; something that you shouldnt mention to anybody because they will look at you peculiarly. But it's hard to keep such a shameful secret for long because people wont believe forever that you are just spending your time fishing and looking for a wholesome job. And if they do, some lousy do-gooder is bound to go out and try to find one for you. The last one I had offered to me was helping pack watermelons which I considered for awhile as I was getting fed up with sitting around the river all the time. But then it was explained to me that I wouldnt really be a watermelon packer, only an assistant watermelon packer, drawing half the pay of a genuine, experienced watermelon packer; and then I had to listen to this fellow talk patronizingly to me for quite a while on how he might could teach me before the season was out all the intricacies of full-fledged watermelon packing, so then I said to hell with it, and came back out to the river and decided I had rather be a sneaky writer again. . . .

Yours, Mac Hyman

When the Atlantic Monthly Press returned the typescript of The Recruits *to Brown, they enclosed, through an oversight, the confidential reports of their readers. These reports, though tentative in their appraisal of the book, were encouraging. A total of four publishers, perhaps five, were to turn down the book before the late Robert Linscott, editor at Random House, discovered its possibilities. Almost a year passed between Hyman's completion of the book and its final acceptance.*

To James Oliver Brown, from Route 3, Cordele, August 7, 1953.

Dear Jim,

Since I got these reports and letters the other day, I have been going back through those parts of THE RECRUITS that I have here, trying to see what I could do with it. . . .

Of course, in doing what I propose to do, it will be nothing but slapstick, "verbal cartoons" as one of them put it, all the way through. My inclination, having begun finally to take Will and Ben fairly seriously as I did in the later sections, is to go back and build everything toward that level instead of vice-versa, but it is fairly obvious that nobody is particularly interested in this angle of it—it is always the slapstick, the falling off fences and such things that anybody thinks is funny. And of course my primary interest right now is to get published and get a start. It doesnt seem that I stand much chance of that if I indulge my own so-called literary taste in the matter; looking through these criticisms and from others that I have heard, it seems that the one consistent thing about them is that every time I try to examine some idea seriously with these two characters, somebody raises an objection. . . . In other words, there seems to be pretty much of an agreement that anything serious—even humorously serious—is out of taste here, and I have no doubts that this is true. On the other hand, though, I am not too wild over the idea of being a gag writer exclusively—like any other poor fool I feel that I want to write Literature with a capital L, that I want to be taken a little bit seriously in time anyhow; and I worry over the fact that if we do happen to get this published, will it cut down on my chances of ever publishing anything serious? (I dont mean necessarily solemn-serious; I mean humorously or any other kind of serious work which is not just plain foolishness as this one is.) Will I get tagged as strickly a gag or comic writer, and nothing else, and have to do That kind of thing forever to get published? Of course maybe that is all I can do, but I somehow cant admit it to myself—and like other fools, even though I *know* that writing is probably nothing but entertainment anyhow, that "Art is a lie," as Tolstoy says,* I somehow dont believe a word of it—or maybe it is I just *wont* believe it, I dont know about that. Anyhow, this bothers me. If I start out with this thing as nothing but jokes, it seems somehow or other to imply that this is all it is worth, that I admit it, and that I am forever surrendering my right to ask any more of it. This might all be a lot of foolishness, but I wonder about it just the same. Honest to God, it is too hard a work to make a job out of it—and if I have to always simply look at it as a job, as nothing else, I'm afraid I'll never get much satisfaction out of it anyhow. I mean I like money as much as the next fellow, and certainly need it, and I damn well need to get published after all this time, but I dont think that is going to be enough in itself. . . .

Yours, Mac

WESTERN UNION

1954 MAR 30 AM 8 21
SY. NC236 NL PD-NEW YORK NY 30
PROF WILLIAM BLACKBURN
DUKE UNIVERSITY DURHAM NCAR
JUST RECEIVED CONTRACT TO PUBLISH NOVEL RANDOM HOUSE MAY I DEDICATE IT TO YOU EVERYBODY HAPPY BILL ROSE [STYRON] AND I DRUNK. ALL SEND REGARDS

MACK HYMAN

* Tolstoy gives a highly personal version of this critical commonplace: a work of art is a "lie" when it fails to transmit feelings which unite men in brotherhood. See his *What Is Art?*, trans. Aylmer Maude (Indianapolis, 1960), xvii, 149.

To William Styron, from Route 3, Cordele, April 9, 1954.

Dear Bill,

Have been meaning to write ever since I got back and tell you how much fun I had around at your place before I left and so on, but I've been so damned busy since I got back here, I really havent had the time. . . . This is the first day I havent worked all day since I got back—what I am having to do is write the last part of the novel over, moving my two so-called heroes to Georgia on maneuvers rather than Korea, and I finally finished the first draft of it yesterday, about thirty damned thousand words in six days. I feel like Hatcher or somebody. Have been going out to the river and staying there most of the day which is as good a place as I can find to write. Nobody to bother with you, no noise from the children and so on, and when you dont care to be writing, you can loaf secretly and not feel half so guilty about it because nobody will ever know the difference.

Incidentally, the morning after I left your place I was so goddamned sick I couldnt see straight. Had to be down at Random House about nine-thirty, was still sick and not half sober, and finally just gave up trying to hear what anybody said to me—just sat there like an idiot and tried to appear very aloof about it all. You can tell Comrade Rose I blame it on her hot-dog—I think that was the finishing touch. Did have a fine time up there, though; they were a nice bunch of people. Got a kick out of [J. P.] Marquand particularly; he seemed in the little bit I talked with him to be a lot of fun and everything.

Around here, things are about the same, except that I have, thank the Lord, turned down that lousy job I was going to take,* and now do not have to apologize for it to anybody. My folks have seen to it that the news has spread around that I might finally get something published, so I am [at] least not the town bum any longer, which can really get to making

* At Warner Robins Air Force Base, eighteen miles south of Macon.

some difference after a bit. It might seem quite easy to rise above the opinions and so on of all around you, but as a matter of fact, it's a pretty hard thing to do. It had even gotten down to the point that I could almost blow my top when some negro would ask, and probably very innocently, why I wasnt working at the store, or something along that line. I drew all sorts of sly insinuations out of it—and a lot of them were there too—and was coming pretty close to hating everybody around me. Anyhow, am hoping that that is over for awhile, if things work out. If I must be a freak around here, at least there is a chance of being now a profitable freak, and that seems to be the difference. Already I have been able to detect some of the change (and this is of course on nothing more than the news that I have a contract)—whereas before I was regarded as certainly lazy and probably crazy (the condition I came back from New York in that time still hovers around), now I might be just "eccentric" and get by with it. I know you have been through all this before and probably felt a good bit of the same business, but I am kind of enjoying the change—now I can go out and write without feeling it is a complete waste of time—and I am getting a kick out of gloating over it.

How is the new book coming? * From the outline of it you gave me, or told me, when I was there before, I couldnt get too much idea about it, of course. I've learned not to go by that too much with you anyhow. I remember a long time ago —the first time I was in New York—you told me you had an idea for a story and said, "It's about this older man that falls in love with this younger girl," and then asked me how I liked it. And naturally I wanted to know, "Well, what happens?" and you didnt have much of an answer for that; you said, "Well, that's all there is to it," but I still remember the story because it turned out to be a pretty damned good one, I thought. It was the one where they were passing by Potters

* *Set This House on Fire* (1960).

Island (is that it?) at the end. So your outlines really dont tell too much. So, how is it coming?

We're still looking forward to your coming down this summer. G. and I might be going down to Fla. for a week sometimes toward the end of this month if I can get this revision off by then, and get somebody to keep the children and so on. When you all come down, though, what I thought we could do is take a boat trip up the river. We can get Daddy's boat and maybe one other, take off some morning with some beer and sandwiches, ski and swim every once in awhile, and make a day out of it. G. and I did it once this summer and had a right big time of it. Once you leave the populated section, you go into these narrow channels through the woods and dont see anybody for a hell of a long time. The day we went, we got as far as Montezuma, about thirty miles off, before we ever turned around. It was right enjoyable.

Let me hear from you if you get the chance. Give Rose my regards, and remember my offer still stands. As soon as I make a big fat fortune out of this book, I'll hire you doing proofs or something for me.

Yours, Mac

To William Blackburn, from Route 3, Cordele, April 9, 1954.

Dear Dr. Blackburn,

. . . Have been having to do some revision on the last part of the book, and as they want it back before the end of the month, I have had to write some thirty thousand words in the past six days. Not that I wasnt damned glad to do it, though. It's the first time in my life I've really been able to write and think there was any possibility much in getting published, and God knows, I'm enjoying it. I go out to the river every morning and work there all day, and it has been pretty satisfying to me.

What happened was, the last fourth of the book is in Korea, and everybody, including myself now, thought that it was probably dated, that it was not consistent with the rest of the novel and so on, so I am having to do it over. So instead of Korea, I'm using maneuvers in Georgia which would not be too much difference to a lot of people, I guess. . . .

Anyhow, it has all been a mighty pleasant surprise, as you could imagine. I had already practically run out of money and hope, and I had a job starting at an airbase nearby that week, thinking maybe I could possibly write another novel in my off hours, when I got a call from the agent asking if I couldnt come up there again, which I was damn well reluctant to do. But he was encouraging, so I scraped up my last hundred dollars to get a ticket there and back, just taking the chance that they might give me a contract and could advance me enough money to get through the next month until I received a check from my job. So you can imagine my delight when I got there and found not only a contract but an advance of fifteen hundred dollars, and a promise of more if I need it, and all sorts of enthusiasm (whether it was real or not I cant say) over the novel itself. It really was kind of unbelievable and I haven't yet gotten used to the idea. Not only do I not have to take that job, but I can write and not feel that I am wasting my time anymore. And there even seems a possibility that I might can make a little money out of it. Bennett Cerf is going to endorse it as "the funniest book he has read in ten years" which ought to sell a few copies whether it is or not. Anyhow it was all quite flattering to me and we're all pretty happy about it. It still does not seem possible as I had begun to feel that I never would be published and was just writing from habit, but it might work out now after all. There is at least a better chance. It really does seem peculiar though that I would not get a break of any sort until I was right down to the point where it was actually a question of eating the next month, but I'm not holding any resentment against the Lord Almighty about it or anything. I'm pleased enough that I am willing to let bygones be bygones, and He and I can bury the hatchet for awhile.

Will send you my copy of the novel as soon as I finish up this last part as it will probably be quite a while before I get the proofs and so on. I hope I havent built it all up so big, though, that you will be disappointed. It actually is not as much as I have made it sound like probably—they were enthusiastic over the *selling* possibilities I think, instead of from the literary point of view. Not that that matters too much to me right now. Mainly I am interested in getting money to be able to write on for awhile whether I am tagged as a commercial writer or not. But that is another very peculiar thing about it all—everybody else that read it kept looking at it from the *literary* angle, for God's sake. Kept wanting to send chapters of it to New World writing and such places. Lots of encouragement but the same old line that it wouldnt sell. So I really dont know what to think anymore; if there is a distinction, and there usually is, it seems, I dont know whether it is artistic, in quotes, or commercial, in quotes. But one good thing is, I guess, that I have reached the point that I dont really give too much of a damn. They can think of it as whatever they want as long as they publish it. . . .

Yours, Mac

To Robert N. Linscott, from Route 3, Cordele, April 22, 1954.

Dear Mr. Linscott:
. . . I'm really enjoying all this now. The news has got around that I might get a book published, and I am known as

probably the best writer in Cordele, Georgia, and feel pretty flattered about it. People even talk to me about it. I was talking to this carpenter not long ago and we had a literary chat and everything—he wanted to know if I had heard about this writer named Hemingblaze that had two airplane crashes in one day.* It seemed to tickle hell out of him. So now I am really not a bum anymore because everybody knows that Mickey Spillane makes money, and who knows? maybe I can too—so I go around looking people straight in the eye, and having a big time out of it. . . .

Yours, Mac

The title finally given the book was the suggestion of Bennett Cerf, then president of Random House. Lew Miller, kind-hearted sales manager of the firm, noticed that the hens and dogs on Pa Stockdale's farm, which are described as being tied up around the yard at the beginning of the book, have not been watered by late the next day.

To Robert N. Linscott, from Route 3, Cordele, April 24, 1954.

Dear Mr. Linscott:

Received both your letters today, the one about watering the chickens and the one about the title, NO TIME FOR SERGEANTS. Have been brooding over the title, as you suggested, and like the sound of it and everything very much. I dont know that I quite understand it, though. Does it mean that Will and Ben have no time to bother with worrying about ever becoming Sergeants themselves, or that they have no time to pay attention to Sergeants and their orders, etc., or that the time covered in the book, when they are around, is

---

* Hemingway and his wife Mary were involved in two crashes within a period of about twenty-four hours near Murchison Falls, Victoria Nile, Uganda.

not a very good time from the Sergeant's point-of-view? I got to wondering about the different ways you could look at it, and really am not sure which one it means; but maybe the fact that different interpretations can be put on it makes it more provocative or something, which it certainly seems to be. I would like to know, though, how Mr. Cerf means it. If somebody asks me about it, I want to be able to come back at them with a real snappy answer so that they will look like a fool for asking, instead of my looking like a fool for not being able to answer. I do like the sound of it a lot, though, and my wife thinks it's the best one she's heard yet; and I think so myself. . . .

I never really thought about watering the chickens and dogs, and am glad you pointed it out. Please thank Mr. Miller for me; it can be corrected just at the place he suggested. On page 14, in the second paragraph, if you would make the sentence read: "I played the harp awhile and raked up around the front while he set there next to the post with the gun across his lap; then I went out and watered the chickens and the dogs that was tied up, and then we both set around for a couple of hours, and I really did get right tired of it all before it was over." * I think that should cover it all right. . . .

Sincerely, Mac

To James Oliver Brown, from Route 3, Cordele, May 14, 1954.

Dear Jim:

. . . I would like to have one [another novel] well on the way and know what I am going to try to do with it before this one comes out if I can. Maybe then I can become involved with it to the extent that anything said about this one, if

* This sentence is in the first printing of the text, pp. 19–20.

anybody says anything about it at all, wont affect anything I might would have done otherwise. I dont mean that I am afraid I will have anything special to live up to, or anything like that, as I have never been wild on the subject of the novel anyhow, but I have noticed that there is a tendency to try to live up to anything that is said about you. I mean, if somebody said you were the biggest liar in the state of Georgia, you might try to start trying to live up to that too, and I dont want to be caught in something like that if I can help it. I would like to rest on my laurels all right, but first I want some laurels to rest on, and God knows, one dinky novel wont be too comfortable, even though I have sweated that out many a year too. Anyhow, right now I plan to try to forget this one and get on with something else because I really have a kind of horror of coming down to the point where I have to keep wondering how I did the last story, and will I do as well again, and living in something that way that should best be forgotten and ignored if I ever expect to do anything with writing in my life. In a way, it might be best living in a place like Cordele for that matter. There are disadvantages, of course, but there is not much danger that you will spend all your time talking to people about your last story, and other stories, because nobody cares anyhow. So the only thing left to do is write another one and that is the only real satisfaction anyhow. . . .

Yours, Mac

In 1950, Max Steele won the $10,000 Harper's Award for his novel Debby (*now in paperback entitled* The Goblins Must Go Barefoot). *For about five years, he lived in Paris, where he served as an advisory editor of* The Paris Review. *His friendship with Hyman began when Steele wrote him, unofficially, praising "The Hundredth Centennial." For two* *or three years after his return to this country, Steele taught story writing at the University of North Carolina, Chapel Hill. He returned to UNC in 1966 as writer-in-residence and is now head of the creative writing program. His collection,* Where She Brushed Her Hair and Other Stories, *appeared in 1968.*

To Max Steele, from Route 3, Cordele, May 24, 1954.

Dear Mr. Steele,

I had just had a bad day of writing the other day when I received your letter and it perked me up to the extent that I went back and did what I thought was a fairly decent piece of work. Thanks a lot for all the mighty nice things you had to say about my story; I appreciate [it] very much, particularly the fact that you went out of your way to write what was to me such a mighty fine letter. I could reciprocate by saying far more about some of your own work, but I'm afraid you might think I was just trying to be obliging, and that would never do. I had just read your story in *Discovery* * a few weeks before, though, and did consider it as a kind of coincidence. By the way, I used to hear of you from another fellow from Greenville, Tom Greet, who is now teaching, I think. I don't know whether he knew you or just knew *of* you, but I think I might have to write him about hearing from you. He writes, too, or did at that time, and it's a good chance for me to fill him up with envy.

It's true that I have been at work on a novel, in fact have just finished it up. It should be out on the Fall List, they say, even though I am [not] quite sure of just what that is, and I am looking forward to it as it is the first thing I have ever been able to sell at all. I wrote one other novel that was lousy and sent it to a publisher but he didnt want it, and when I got it back and looked it over, I couldnt much blame him, so I put

* "Hear the Wind Blow," *Discovery*, No. 3 (New York, 1954), 197–213.

it away and started on this other one, which I signed a contract for (with an advance too, by God, which was the first cent I have ever received out of writing in my life) about two months ago. It is to be called NO TIME FOR SERGEANTS, published by Random House, but I am afraid you will be disappointed in it if you were expecting anything because it is strictly a comedy and nothing much else, and about the only thing I can say for it at the time is that it was at least publishable, which so much of my stuff has not been. So there really is not too much to it; it's not even serious humor, I dont think, but at least I had fun writing it and it will at least give me a chance to do some other writing for awhile instead of taking other jobs here and there. For the past few years I have had to jump from one job to the other with three years in the Air Force as a recallee and could write only in my spare time, so it seems to me now something of a luxury to be able to write when I want to, and also of course to be able to tell the many people who wonder out loud to me why I am not holding a steady job now to step to hell. I suppose you went through all that, though, didn't you? Anyhow, the signing of the contract for the novel and good remarks you have made about my story have made me feel something like a whiz all of a sudden so that things dont look so hopeless now after all. . . .

I envy you being in Paris. I like it here but I like to move around every once in awhile and I have never been to Europe at all. If I can make any money out of this book, though, I might finally make a try at it myself. It sounds like a good life from all I can hear of it. I have a couple of children, though, one of them getting close to school age, and I hate to up-root them, even with this non-segregation business coming along. Anyhow, I would like to, and if I ever do, I'll buy you a quart of whatever you like best for all the nice things you have said.

Sincerely yours, Mac Hyman

To James Oliver Brown, from Route 3, Cordele, June 1, 1954.

Dear Jim:

. . . Just got back this week-end and had news from Bob Linscott that I would be getting proofs about June 3 which sounds very good to me. Have been piddling around with some other stuff, but I guess I will hold up now until I have this all out of the way and don't have to bother about it any longer. Do things still look all right to you? I never get over the feeling the whole deal might be cancelled at any moment.

I hate to bother you with the financial business but I would appreciate it if you would drop a hint or something about the rest of that advance because I am really having to step very lightly now.

Yours, Mac

To William Styron, from Route 3, Cordele, July 16, 1954.

Dear Bill,

I was just going to write to you to find out if you all were going to be able to come down this summer when I got your letter. Tell Rose we're mightly happy for her; G. is now in the same condition again, expecting sometimes around January,* I guess, and if you all could have made it, they would probably have a bang-up time discussing symtoms and things. That's a good idea anyhow; why don't you all get on a plane and fly down to Atlanta—that won't hurt her—we'll meet you there and bring you here, and they can sit with their hands folded over their stomachs and talk and we can get in this trailer I got yesterday (instead of the powder-blue Cadillac), hitch it up to the back of the car and take off for Florida for

---

* Tom Hyman was born January 17, 1955.

awhile. I'm thinking about doing that before the summer is out anyhow; I've been wanting a trailer for a long time and yesterday I talked the bank into lending me another [sum?] to get this second hand one I found—if I don't want to bum around in it, I can use it for an office of some kind around here—drag it down in the woods where the children can't find it.

How are you feeling about being a potential legal father now? Probably you have no more feeling about it than I did. As for myself, I just don't have any feeling for unborn children anyhow—G. does; by the time she's two months gone she usually knows their personality and everything but I have to see them in the flesh and be around them awhile before I even believe they exist. But after that time, of course, they kind of begin to grow on you—I think you'll like it. . . .

It was flattering to hear Marquand's report on it; * tell him when I read the next thing he writes I am going to think it's absolutely first-rate too. Actually I hate for anybody to hear good reports about it before they read it, though; when they do they're bound to be disappointed because it really is just a comedy—there's not a serious thing in it—you can't find a symbol if you hunt for one—it's just a joke book by Mac (Ha! Ha!) Hyman, writ for the purpose of publishing something to try to get started with so I dont have to take any more lousy jobs.

By the way, I got a nice, long letter from Max Steele on the Paris *Review* about that short story, but he also disclaims any responsibility of authority, and I havent heard anything else since. Do they always take that long to reject or take a story? They've had that thing since Feb. now—five months. Getting impatient about it. By the way, I read your review in it—I was

* The late J. P. Marquand, as a member of the editorial board of the Book-of-the-Month Club, sat with the officials of Random House when they conferred with Hyman on March 31 (see letter to Styron, April 9, 1954, above). In a letter now lost, Styron sent Hyman news of Marquand's report to the Club.

up in Durham a couple of weeks ago for a day or so—and Blackburn had it. Got a kick out of it—especially that about "Young writers should write and not drink too much." *

Hope your novel is coming along. I've been piddling around a good bit but mainly jumping back and forth between one and the other, unable to make up my mind which to work on. I'd like to have one well on the way by the time that this one comes out so that I won't, as you say, get stuck on No. 2. But it won't be number two with me, come to think of it—it'll be number three; number one is still sitting in the desk drawer where it has remained in disgrace since the first time it was sent back to me. This throws a whole new light on the subject—my batting average so far as novels go is fifty per cent, short stories, zero. So I couldnt get too taken away with things, I don't think, even if I wanted to, being as I can never forget such facts as that. . . .

Mac

To Max Steele, from Route 3, Cordele, July 30, 1954.

Dear Max:

. . . Anyhow, I have had right good luck with the novel since I last wrote you—they called me up about a month ago and told me that the Book-of-the-Month Club was going to take it as one of their dual selections for October; so, even though this might be some kind of literary insult, I will at least get a nice little pot of money for it, something for which I have developed a good bit of reverence over the past few years. It means I will take no more lousy jobs for awhile anyhow and I can now loaf around the middle of town with-

* See Peter Matthiessen and George Plimpton, "Interview with William Styron," *Paris Review* (Spring, 1954), 43–57. Collected in *Writers at Work: The Paris Review Interviews*, introd. by Malcolm Cowley (New York, 1958), 267–82.

out worrying because nothing on God's earth makes the local folk's eyes gleam like the thought of money, and instead of being a bum, I am out gathering material that I can probably make some more dough on, all of which is now right pleasant. Only I don't know how long I plan to stay around here now—I have bought me a second hand trailer and probably as soon as my wife gets up from having number three child, I'll hook it up to the car and we'll go somewhere else for a little while. I don't know, though. But if we don't, I can still use it for a kind of office which I am doing now. It's parked down in the pecan grove right next to the hog pen which is a very good place because if you ever get a little too taken away with the prose, you can glance out the side window and see them in all their mud-wallowing contempt and it brings you back to earth in a hurry. In fact, in too much of a hurry sometimes, I'm afraid. I am now piddling around trying to get moving on this other thing I wanted to do, but am getting pretty disgusted with my progress. How is your stuff coming along? If the fishing village helps, I'd be anxious to know. I would take off for one myself—I think I am getting kind of sorry around here.

As for the 40 published intellectuals at the Cafe Tournon, I know what you mean, but I keep contrasting them with the hogs, and at least they have theories. I think I would *like* some theories for a change. It would wipe out a lot of silly ones I have myself, I think, because if I heard what I thought being said by somebody I didn't particularly like, I probably wouldn't think it anymore. But I do know what you mean; still, hog-heaven is not exactly with the hogs either, I don't think.

By the way, you've got me puzzled. You say in your letter that you all are "glad to have the chance to publish it"— meaning my story. Do you mean they're *going* to publish it? I was just wondering. I could read it both ways, and didn't know which it meant, and being as, outside of this novel I have, I have never yet had a story accepted by anybody, I'm right anxious to know. If you have a chance, drop me a line about it, will you? I'd appreciate it a lot.

It makes me feel good that you are interested in my novel. It flatters hell out of me, but, as I said before, it really is just a comedy and nothing else, and even though I was proud to get it published and especially proud to get some money out of it, I put no great stock in it. I had fun writing it, though—it was a kind of relief from other things at the time, but seriously, I do not swear by it or anything, and at times I am very afraid I will get stuck with that kind of thing because I had my first luck with it. But anyhow I hope you enjoy it and I appreciate your wanting to read it.

Thanks again for the letter. I enjoy hearing from you very much.

Mac

To Robert N. Linscott, from Route 3, Cordele, September 13, 1954.

Dear Mr. Linscott:

Came back Friday from the beach in Florida where I didn't get anything done but one short story typed up, and I am now back home again, trying hard to get nothing done here too. But there have been many distractions—dove season is in for a twenty day period and the elections have just gotten over with and we have finally elected for Governor the one of the nine candidates who promises in every speech to go to jail to uphold segregation in the schools if necessary, and I think that the picture of him running the state from behind prison bars has caught the imagination of the people of Georgia, so he won by a landslide. . . .

As ever, Mac

To Max Steele, from Route 3, Cordele, September 17, 1954.

Dear Max:

I finally got [straightened?] out about the story—got a check yesterday which I am right proud of, though not so proud not to have already cashed it, and am now looking forward to seeing it in print. I appreciate your writing to them about it; I was really getting right confused. It seems that a letter got lost or something, which caused it all. Anyhow, I'm glad I got in touch with you. . . .

I'm getting a little bit of news on the novel now, which is a new kind of experience for me, so that I get kind of a kick out of it, in a way. Some of them like it and some don't; I suppose that is to be expected, but I find myself suddenly totally without character of any sort, in the fact that I find myself liking people who like my book, whether they're bastards or not, and disliking those who don't, saints or otherwise. . . . Is this natural or do I approach this thing wrong somehow? And another thing that bothers me is this: I never took this novel seriously at all; it was something I had fun writing and kind of threw together in the hopes of finally getting something published, and that was all, and that was the way I have felt about it. And I still feel that way about it, but it seems that suddenly I don't like for anybody *else* to feel that way about it. Which puts me into a very phony situation. It's something like "I can curse my wife, but you had better not try it." But anyhow I am kind of enjoying it all as a new experience. I know you have been through most of this, though, so probably it's old stuff to you anyhow.

Thanks again for writing to New York. I hope your own work is coming along better than mine is at the moment; this damned piddling around gets on my nerves. Let me hear from you if you get the chance. . . .

As Ever, Mac

*To James Oliver Brown, from Route 3, Cordele, October 4,
1954.*

Dear Jim,

   . . . I never thought of television at all; it just never occurred to me that they could use it. I'm glad you all did. It
seems to be a good break.

From the writing angle of it, though, I imagine they might
have a right hard time getting it into any kind of shape so that
it won't be just pure slap-stick when you see it on a stage.
They must have some ideas about how to do it, though, if
they are willing to offer money. But the problem remains, as
far as I see it, in getting the humor into it because about
nine-tenths of it comes from the fact that Will is telling the
story, you're seeing it all through his eyes, and the reader sees
one thing happening while Will tries to tell about something
else. The only way you could so do this, it seems to me, is to
bring out in dialogue at the very beginning how Will thinks,
how he sees things, and this can get to be pretty unbelievable.
I know because I did a little of it in third person one time to
see how it would go, and where you can have Will toss off
some very stupid remark in his mind, when you put the
quotes around it, or have it said, it is not believable anymore.
I don't know why, but it just isn't. I know that many times
when I was writing it, I would put down things in dialogue,
and when they didn't feel right, I would throw them into a
kind of narrative form, and then they seemed a little more
acceptable. Just for example, in the first of the book when
they come out to draft Will, if you put McKinney's discussion
with Pa and Will into dialogue, it becomes in a way more
unbelievable, even though you can approach what they call
"reality" a lot better this way. As a matter of fact, one of the
things about getting something like this done is to keep it
from being real in the first place. But that seems confusing—

let me put it this way. Once I wrote the scene where the boys in the draft are kidding Will and Ben and getting the man to shoot them with the needle a lot harder than the rest of them. Now the problem in a place like this is to keep anybody from actually *seeing* the needle. Because if you do bring this down to the level of reality, and see the scene for what it is, the cruelty behind it, the actual pain and so on, it's damn well not funny anymore. So the trick is to have the incident happen without anyone actually seeing it, or feeling it—in other words, just kind of the opposite of "reality". But of course this can be accomplished in third person too, which is about the way the stage would have to do it, if there is a pretty strong "opinion" or "director" or something behind it. For example, in so many of the movies that John Houston directs, you get a feeling of a live camera behind it all that really wants to tell you something, even though it is doing it really without comment. It will need something like that in the background, it seems to me, so you get the sense of somebody telling you a story that has certain values set up at the beginning, so that, for example, the needle itself isn't important. I know all of this is pretty dull and confused, and I damn well don't want to discourage anybody from trying to put it on television or in the movies, but I do think it will be right hard trying to dramatize, and think that there will have to be a few changes made. . . .

I've been kind of enjoying the reviews even though they are a puzzle to me most of the time. Of course, Mauldin's was right interesting to me,* and I decided that the trouble was that he was one of these professional veterans, suffering from some kind of battle fatigue, which is understandable. You take a man who goes all the [way] through a war with the danger of having his drawing pencil flip up and hit him in the

* "What annoys me about 'No Time for Sergeants' is that Hyman is a better humorist than he thinks; he doesn't need time-tested formulas." See Bill Mauldin, "Now See Here, Mr. Hyman," *Herald Tribune Book Review*, October 3, 1954, p. 8.

eye and spilling ink all over his uniform, his nerves are bound to be right ragged when it is over, and he doesn't want to see any such serious subjects taken so lightly. But then I calmed down and said to hell with it and decided that was a right unfair way of looking at it, and now I don't really care except for the implication that I borrowed the idea from THE GOOD SOLDIER SCHWEIK, which I have never read or even heard of before up until about six months ago. Or DERE MABLE either for that matter; I did read PRIVATE HARGROVE, but that was about ten years ago and I don't even remember the thing. So if I'm going to be accused of plagiarism, I would at least like to have stolen from books that I have read anyhow; it seems too mysterious or something this way.

Anyhow, I can't see why there is anything in it to *upset* anybody. The whole thing is only a joke anyhow, and even though I do have a few little digs that I meant to be taken kind of seriously, the idea that these are anything much other than characteaures is kind of far-fetched anyhow. But next time I get onto a book, I want it to be one that I can stand by, so to speak, and say "This is the way things are," and not have to keep hedging about. Because this one is, as Faulkner said of SANCTUARY, a kind of cheap idea, and I hope that my vanity doesn't put me into the position of having to think of it as anything more. Anyhow, through this, I might not have so much trouble getting published next time and I won't have to be taking any more lousy jobs for a while and now that I have a chance to get started, I think I might be reconciled to the thought of not being able to write, if I can't. Because now I couldn't blame it on anything but myself. . . .

Yours, Mac

To James Oliver Brown, from Route 3, Cordele, early October, 1954.

Dear Jim:

. . . As for going out to Hollywood,* I wouldn't mind doing that at all. Would probably like it, as a matter of fact. And as Faulkner says, "They can't hurt you unless you're willing to be hurt." †—So I might enjoy it. Anyhow, if it comes up, I'm willing. . . .

Yours, Mac

To James Oliver Brown, from Route 3, Cordele, October 10, 1954.

Dear Jim:

. . . As for doing a play, I had just as soon as I am not getting any writing done now anyhow, and it might get me started back again. I have never thought of the novel in terms of a play, though; it just never occurred to me you could make one out of it. And it really would have to be a job of collaboration because I don't know anything about writing for the stage at all. I doubt if I have seen more than three professional plays in my life and as well as I remember, I had a hard time sitting through those. But that is another thing that might be worth learning and I would be glad to try it. If people are willing to produce it, they must think people will go to see it. I, personally, would never go to see a play with a bunch of GI's in it, but, as I say, I'm no judge of it. . . .

That Tea at the library is this afternoon and I am steeling myself to suffer through it.‡ But I'm going to it and then I'm going to the one in Atlanta because of friends and family up

* As a consultant on filming *No Time for Sergeants.*
† To the question "Can working for the movies hurt you own writing?" Faulkner once replied, "Nothing can injure a man's writing if he's a first-rate writer." See *Writers at Work: The Paris Review Interviews* (New York, 1958), 125.
‡ Given by the Fine Arts Club in the Carnegie Library.

there, and then I don't think I'm ever again going to go through with such things. It really gives me the horrors. I'm supposed to write personal things in the books of people I don't even know and they get insulted if what you write isn't clever or something. And to show you what it can amount to —there's going to be relatives from both my parents' families there, and last year I went to a family reunion of just my grandmother's side of the family and there were over three hundred cousins of various degrees. Multiply that by all the other sides and try to write something personal for each and every and see what you have. No sir, this one and the one in Atlanta,* and I'm through forevermore.

I'm glad I'm not in your shoes right now, though. If I were handling all that, I would probably just say "Certainly," to everybody who had an idea and find myself involved in God knows what.

It all really is kind of amazing, though, isn't it? I guess eight months ago if somebody had offered five hundred dollars for the whole works and all the rights, I would have been for snapping it up in a second. Anyhow, I'm still waiting for it to fizzle out, and if every dealer returned every book right now and they'd burn them in the middle of Times Square, I'd still think it had been lucky beyond all bounds.

As ever, Mac

To William Blackburn, from Route 3, Cordele, October 12, 1954.

Dear Dr. Blackburn,

. . . So far, though, I've only gotten three or four bad reviews against about fifty good ones, which is better than I

---

* Hyman autographed copies of his book at Rich's Book Shop in Atlanta on October 18.

expected. A woman in Savannah gave me a bad one; * and Bill Mauldin burned me up with his in the New York *Tribune* by implying that I stole the whole thing from THE GOOD SOLDIER SCHWEIK, which I have never read; and the *New Yorker* kind of disgusted me by saying nothing about the book but coming out with some asinine little remark that I "seemed to think I was a very funny writer" † which I thought was pretty ridiculous because how in the hell could somebody try to write humor, and *not* think it was funny. And because of all people who think themselves funny, I guess that bunch of sterile sophisticates picking around with their manacured nails in the completely yellow bile after one of their cocktail parties where they sit around saying priceless things to each other think they are probably the greatest group of caustic wits ever assembled in an air-conditioned building. Which only just goes to prove what Styron told me before and which I didn't believe—that fifty good ones don't matter, the one you remember is the bad one.

But I really don't mind the other bad one I got, from some place in Iowa.‡ The fellow just didn't like it, said so, said why, and it's all right by me. I can certainly understand a lot of people not liking it—a hell of a lot of publishing houses didn't; there is no reason why all the reviewers should. And as far as their calling it a *burlesque* or *farce*, or something like that, that doesnt bother me at all—in fact, I hadnt even thought about it before you mentioned it, mainly, I guess, because that's what I think of it too. As a matter of fact, that's the way I've described it to anybody who asked me what it was. But I don't have any terrific amount of vanity about this

* See Katherine Scardino, "Humorous Saga of a Noble Cracker," Savannah *News*, September 5, 1954: "His Will Stockdale rings perfectly true. . . . He needs blue-pencilling and pointing up, nice as he is."

† *The New Yorker*, October 9, 1954, pp. 182–83: "Something about Mr. Hyman's manner of telling his story indicates that he considers himself a very funny writer."

‡ See Peter Grevas, "Hillbilly Draftee Fails In Attempt at Army Humor," Davenport *Times*, October 3, 1954.

book anyhow, so they can think what they like about that. But when it comes to taking cracks at me, personally, I resent the hell out of it because I havent put myself up for exibition yet, and that, by God, passes outside the realm of "critical license" or whatever you call it, and I forget we're talking about books, and get ready to step outside.

But, as I say, in general, things still look pretty good. I understand that they printed thirty thousand copies, so I guess they'll kind of have to push it to get rid of them. Also, some movie companies seem interested (they're mainly worried about getting cooperation from the Air Force, it seems), but now my agent is thinking of withdrawing it from the movies because he says he is being swamped (his word, not mine) by producers who want to make a play out of it, which could make some money, I guess, if it were successful. Also there has been an offer from TV, the US Steel Hour, to dramatize it on there. I don't know whether or not this has been accepted—I keep out of it all as much as possible. I don't know anything about the business end of it and don't really care too much what they do with it. Naturally, I'd like the money, whatever they decide to do, and will certainly cooperate along that line as there is no telling when I'll ever make any-more, and it will leave me free for awhile. . . .

As far as the Book Party went, it was plenty brutal, that and what they called a "book review" a couple of weeks before. But there were many folks feelings involved, family and friends and friends of family, and I couldnt very well refuse and everybody (they did have a big crowd too, at both of them) seemed to have a nice time, and I discussed literature with people who have never read four books before, and even though I really did appreciate it, the idea of their wanting to do something and all, I really suffered before it was all over with. I've got one more before me in Atlanta, and that's all. And I mean that's all. I've slid out of the others and intend to do some strong sliding from here on out. It is a kind of strange change, though; from local bum to local celebrity in about six months and in a perverse way, I get kind of a kick out of it. I now hunt on the best land and never am at a loss for an invitation, which is one of the many privileges. But I still appreciate their doing it—of course, it's the idea of the money (rumors are running around that I have already made about two hundred thousand dollars and I don't do anything to stop them; I just give them a little nudge every once in a while) and not the book—most of them havent even read the book and won't like it when they do, but I don't care, really.

12 Oct. 54

Didn't get to finish this because a friend came by for a beer, and then yesterday I went up to Athens to take my kid sister her car. Rode the bus back last night.

Anyhow, we have to be in Atlanta up through the 19th and within a couple of days from that time, I'm expecting on fixing up the trailer and heading up that way for awhile. Will let you know. And of course I'd be mighty happy to come to your class again. I really need to be writing now and maybe it will get me started again.

As ever, Mac

To James Oliver Brown, from Route 3, Cordele, November 7, 1954.

Dear Jim:

. . . I have got myself on a pretty strict schedule now, trying to get started on this next one. Loused the whole schedule up last week by having to take my wife to the doctor one day (in Macon), my Daddy another, and fifty other things that got in my way. This week, though, if the hogs get out, which they manage to do right often, they'll have to stay out until three o'clock which is the time I am setting aside to get them back in. The one I am working on,* the one that Mr. Linscott wrote about, is supposed to be that first one that I wrote—doing it over from the standpoint of one of the characters, which I had piddled around with before. Will write more in detail about it later, after I see where it is going. From what I have down so far, it has no resemblance whatsoever to the first one—I'm not using the same characters or the same theme or anything; so even after I finish re-writing it this time, if I do finish, I'll have to go back and re-write it again, I guess, because the only thing alike in them so far is that the name of the town is spelled the same. I could spend the rest of my life re-writing that same book, it looks like. . . .

As ever, Mac

To *William Blackburn, from Route 3, Cordele, November 13, 1954.*

Dear Dr. Blackburn:

. . . In a way—not really, I don't guess, but I certainly have the feeling sometimes—I wish it would go on and get off the best-seller list and all that (which I don't doubt it will do right soon now) so I could get on to something else. I am really getting kind of tired of the thing. For example, the other day—about a week ago—I was on to something and they called from New York to say that I had to make a decision one way or the other, that there was an offer from a movie company of sixty thousand dollars plus a cut in the movie which could run it up quite a few more thousand, and that I had to decide whether to accept that or not, or take a gamble on this play deal with Maurice Evans which could of course be a complete flop, which would mean I would lose that nice amount from the movie. Anyhow, it all came right

---

* *Take Now Thy Son.*

close to knocking my eyes out—that ungodly sum of money dangling in front of my eyes which have never seen such amounts (I had previously been reprimanding myself for being too optimistic when I thought we might could get fifteen thousand dollars for the screen rights)—especially having to make a quick decision on it that way. But I made it finally—I had to think about thirty minutes, though, and call them back—anyhow, I decided I had just as soon go ahead and gamble with the play idea, because having gambled on all of it as long as I have, there didn't seem to be much sense in stopping at that point. As they say, you shouldn't ever let go of the dice when you're on a lucky streak, and even though I was pretty tempted for a little bit, I decided just to let the bets ride, and give it another roll. All of this is just gravy to me anyhow. So I don't guess I have that much to lose really, either way you look at it.

Anyhow, Maurice Evans has lined up the writers of STALAG 17 * to do the playwriting, and they seem right enthusiastic, so it might go over after all. . . .

You mentioned the Faulkner letter,† and I'll have to admit that it really did make me feel good to think of his going to the trouble and everything. I guess out of all of this—not that the money and that part hasn't meant a lot to me—that that has meant more to me than anything else. I finally even got up nerve to write and thank him for it. I didn't want to impose or anything but I couldn't let him get away with doing me a favor like that and not thanking him, so I went ahead and did it anyhow.

* Donald Bevan and Edmund Trzcinski wrote the stage play of this name. The job of writing the stage version of No Time for Sergeants, however, was finally turned over to Ira Levin.

† Faulkner read proofs of No Time for Sergeants while visiting Robert Linscott in New York. At Linscott's request, he wrote the following comment: "The story of the bomber training flight is one of the funniest stories of war or peace either, of the functioning at its most efficient best of man's invincible and immortal folly, that I have ever read." See advertisement of the book, New York Times, October 13, 1954, p. 29.

Mac and his sisters just before he entered the Army Air Corps in 1943. Mitzi, then a Wesleyan student, later became an actress and director of Atlanta's Pocket Theater. Dinah, the younger sister, became an artist.

Mac and his wife Gwendolyn, who was his high school sweetheart, look over his newly published novel in 1957.

Mac was an outdoorsman from his early youth. Here he is boating with his parents.

Mac at the lectern, Columbia University, 1957.

The 1954 family snapshot at left shows Mac with his cocker spaniel. At right he is photographed with the late Robert Linscott, who was editor at Random House when Mac's novel was accepted for publication.

In February, 1963, five months before his death, Mac appeared on the television program "Meet the Professor" with (from left) William Blackburn, Fred Chappell, William Styron, and Reynolds Price.

Hope the class is coming along. I'm still planning on coming up but I know now I have to wait for awhile. I just hope that by that time I have something at least readable. But this typewriter doesnt seem to realize the luck I had on the other one and still thinks of me as strictly an amateur, which knocks my ego down a bit, and makes me right angry sometimes to find out it is just as hard now as it ever was.

Let me hear from you when you have the chance.

As ever, Mac

To Robert N. Linscott, from Route 3, Cordele, December 3, 1954.

Dear Mr. Linscott:

. . . Excuse the long letter, but I'm all alone down here and my wife has been pregnant about twelve months and has about five more to go, and I haven't written even a little masterpiece in several weeks now, and just wanted to write. Hope everything is going fine with you all. I received the *Encyclopedia* of Mr. Cerf's today and am very happy about it.* Had been to Macon the day before and had bought a copy, so now I've got two and my wife and I can read it at the same time with no trouble.

I saw from some of the copies of NO TIME FOR SERGEANTS that you all had gone into a second printing.† I guess that means you won't get stuck with that first printing, doesn't it? I'm mighty glad to hear it. . . .

Yours, Mac

* Bennett Cerf ran two episodes from *No Time for Sergeants* in *An Encyclopaedia of Modern American Humor* (Garden City, 1954), 290–301.
† Total sales through October, 1968: Random House (hardcover), 220,000 copies. This hardcover edition in recent years sells at an average rate of about 3,000 copies annually. The New American Library, Signet Books (paperback), 2,293,227. No figures are available from the Book-of-the-Month Club.

To James Oliver Brown, from Route 3, Cordele, December 8, 1954.

Dear Jim,

. . . A couple of day ago, two women came by from——
—, Georgia and said they had been working fifteen years on a long novel that was a lot better than *Gone With The Wind;* they had now finished it, even though they wanted to do some cutting, and wanted to know if you would take it. I gave them the story about your being filled up, but told them I would ask you and write to them. They said Margaret Mitchell was going to help them get it published, but then she had to go and get killed,* and they seemed to be pretty disgusted at her about this. . . .

Yours, Mac

To William Blackburn, from Route 3, Cordele, December 27, 1954.

Dear Dr. Blackburn,

. . . I heard from a fellow who said the Paris *Review* with my story in it was out, but I havent seen it as yet. Doubt they'll send me one, even. I guess I'll find a copy one of these day, though. The book is still going right good—they've gone into their seventh printing, I believe—maybe the sixth, though, I'm not sure. Anyhow, they wrote last week and said they now had sold about sixty thousand, had printed ten more thousand and had the eightieth thousand on the presses. So I'm spending the money now—bought Gwendolyn a station wagon, Ford, started buying this house, and gave the chillun quite a Xmas, paid for my trailer, and kept enough back to

* Margaret Mitchell was run down by an automobile in Atlanta and died five days later, August 16, 1949.

live until the next pay-off. Yessir, I like the idea of money fine. I think it's going to come in handy.

Got a card from Styron who says they will be moving up to Conn. after the first of the year. I guess you knew about the house they bought up there, sounds like a mighty nice one.

Hope to see you around the last of next month, if things work out right.

As ever, Mac

P.S. Speaking of your student———and the long haul in front of him, I know what you mean, but it has always seemed to me that something like writing is one of those things that is nobody's fault. If somebody wants to badly enough, he'll kind of have to because nothing else will satisfy him, and he'd be a fool not to stick at it. And if he doesn't want to badly enough, he'll quit sooner or later anyhow. If it weren't a struggle, it wouldn't be worth doing anyhow, more than likely. I personally have no pity much (at least most of the time) for the struggling "artist" and so on. I think they deserve every kick in the teeth they get until failure gets to be the natural thing with them, and then anything that's left, after they've taken enough beatings for awhile, might be worth having. I mean I like to see somebody go at it the way Ben Hogan went at golf, or Ty Cobb at baseball—they're the kind that last, I think, because they've built a strong foundation. Talent, in itself, it seems to me, doesn't amount to too much, if there is even such a thing. I never much doubt that anybody with common sense could write if they tried it—I usually doubt they *will* write, though; that's something else.

But I do know what you mean, having to take the responsibility of advising them and sending them down that long road and everything. I know I would hate to have to do it—I couldn't do it, as a matter of fact. But then, I'm not a teacher, and it's one of those things I can avoid having to do and keep a clear conscience at the same time.

Excuse me for this long diatribe. I get taken away with the sound of my own words sometimes.

M

To James Oliver Brown, from Route 3, Cordele, December 29, 1954.

Dear Jim:

Received your letter of the 27th today, and, as you suggested on the phone to my Sister yesterday, have been ignoring it very hard all day. What happened? Did they finally go ahead and eliminate the idea of the TV show or something without writing about it? Hope so anyhow, if that's what you think would be best—I kind of think so too. I always leave myself sitting in a position so that when something happens I can say I thought so all along, which ought to get pretty irritating to you, but I have wondered myself every once in awhile about the TV show. I know personally that I would never go to see a play, pay the money and everything, if I had already seen something like it on TV—I would go to see something else. On the other hand, though, I don't guess I would even do that. If it was up to me personally, I don't think I would even go to see it at all, if I didn't have something to do with it. Anyhow, I hope it works out all right.

Really, though, I'm not too surprised that they might be having trouble dramatizing the thing. I'll bet the STALAG 17 boys have trouble with it too. The only way I can judge it, of course, is that it will be something like writing it in third person, and, as I say, I've tried that myself, and I know it didn't go so well that way. Maybe they can find the key, though, or something.

I've been sick here lately and haven't done a damn thing. Been over two weeks now. What happened was, I got the old-time flu, then got chilled going duck hunting just as I was getting it, and it hit me right hard. Then I got up too soon, had to go back to bed again; then the next time I got up, it settled in my ear somehow so that I had to have the drum punctured, and then it effected what they call my inner-ear so that I stumbled around drunkenly for about three days, thinking I was losing my mind, before they thought to tell me what the trouble was—that the infection was effecting my equilibrium and so on. Anyhow, I'm still deaf in the right ear, still weak, and so full of penicillin and sulphur (sulfa) pills and what-not that I guess I'll be another two weeks recovering from the medicine. Also, there are complications with my wife and the unborn one—they X-rayed today—so we really feel like a bunch of invalids at the time. . . .

I guess the telephone call yesterday caused some confusion. We weren't here and my Sister had the children, and my oldest one, Gwyn, answered the phone—Sister was outside. Anyhow, when Sister asked her who it was on the phone, Gwyn said she didn't know; she said, "It's just some woman —she asked if Daddy was home and I said No, and she asked if Mama was home, and I said No, and then she said 'Hello' about that much times, and I said 'Hello' back at her, and then all she did was just say, 'Oh, dear, Oh, dear,' for awhile —I think she was just crazy or something." I finally got the message straight, though, and didn't write the letter.

Let me know if there is anything I can do. Hope it works out.

Yours, Mac

P.S. Do you remember a while back when I called you about the fellow who wanted to do a recording of a piece of the book? I doubt if he ever got in touch with you—I think he was going out of town right after that—but in case he does, I can tell you here what I know and maybe it will help. His name is Andy Griffith, and a year or so back he made a record called WHAT IT WAS, WAS FOOTBALL, about a hillbilly who saw his first game, and it was pretty popular everywhere. I don't mean just on selling records in stores, but it was on practically every juke organ in every joint, and for a long time people went around trying to imitate it. I asked a few people about it in New York, though, and it wasn't known up there by anybody I asked. But he later did the same reading on the Ed Sullivan TV show, and later made another record ROMEO AND JULIET that I never heard, but which also sold probably a million, or something like that, because practically everybody else I've talked to has heard it—at least, around here.

Anyhow, he says he has talked to Capital Records and they're all for doing a recording, both sides of the record, of whatever chapter or piece we pick out of the book. Seemed to be right enthusiastic about it and all, and the reason is, as I say, that the character that he portrays is about the same kind as I wrote about; and he thinks it will be a big hit and all.

Anyhow, I personally think it might be worth looking into because if it does amount to anything, it will reach an audience that books or plays or TV never reaches, and it's a hell of a big audience too. You can ask a lot of people around here and places like this who McCarthy or Faulkner or Hemingway is and they won't have the slightest idea, but you mention Andy Griffith and they not only know who he is, they can practically quote his records. I was just thinking that would be a nice audience to have because if they heard him read a chapter or something of it, they might go out and buy the whole thing. . . .

Mac

To William Blackburn, from Route 3, Cordele, January 10, 1955.

Dear Dr. Blackburn,

I can understand how you are somewhat confused over the idea of the play and what they say about the movies too. I read that about Danny Kaye being in the movie version myself and it was a surprise to me too. What they were talking about, though, was that he might be in the movie version when the play is over with, or if the play didnt work, and they decided just to make a movie instead. We're still going ahead with Maurice Evans, though, and I guess they are still planning on doing it this fall. I keep out of it as much as possible —I have complete confidence in my agent, which I feel is justified, and listen pretty much to what he has to say about how to handle the whole thing. As a matter of fact, it turned out pretty lucky that I didnt accept the sixty thousand; got an offer today from Warner Brothers for a hundred thousand (I'm getting to the point where I am not even amazed anymore). Could have gone on with it but of course I'm too far in with Evans and them now to back out on that, even though the papers haven't as yet been signed or anything. Still, it wouldnt have been right to have pulled it away at this late date, so I wouldnt do it. Anyhow, they still offered what they called a pre-production deal whereby I can sign with them— Warner's—now, and if the play is a failure, or does not play more than about three weeks, I can still get the hundred thousand from them. On the other hand, if it runs for over that amount of time, I have to split with Evans and the playwrites, and get only thirty thousand, plus royalties on the play. It's all right complicated—there is also something in the offer to the effect that as long as the play runs, the price Warners will pay will go up until they reach the unbelievable figure of two hundred and fifty thousand. It's all kind of fantastic, but I finally decided I would accept that one because I can still get the play and have some security in case it doesnt succeed. Evans wanted me to turn it down so that he could see about producing the movie later himself, thinking we would all come out better that way, but I couldnt quite see it. I would be gambling a hundred thousand that way and none of the rest of them would be gambling anything except on the play; and I'm in no position to do it. . . .

Still hoping to get up there, but I think I am going to sell the trailer. I dont work in it; usually I end up going out to the river anyhow. The baby is due Jan. 22 and G. is getting pretty tired this time—the other two were seven month babies and she is not used to going this long. Anyhow, after it comes and I see that all is okay, I'll probably be on my way. I would have thought it would be here by now.

Hope all the money figures don't bore you. I just thought you might be interested as it is all so amazing to me. Sweat out turning down one figure and get offered nearly twice as much a month later—it's very peculiar. Incidentally, all of this is not secret or anything—the figures, I mean—but I wouldnt much want it to get out until things are a little more definite. Just accepted it on the phone today, so naturally there could still be hitches in it.

Also, got another good offer from Capitol records for this fellow to record some of it (Andy Griffith—don't know whether you've heard of him or not), which might work into something; and also finally sold the pocket book rights to come out in '56. That was also a right peculiar deal—we had one other with a pocket book company that finally fell through, and then this one came about that pays over twice as much.

But I'll be glad to get it all settled and get it out of my head for awhile. I had made up my mind that with the coming of the New Year, I would forget it and go on with something else, and today is the first time I've thought much about it since. Anyhow, though, maybe this will get rid of it for awhile, and I can go on with this idea I have for the long story or the short novel or whatever it is, and get some writing done for a change.

Anyhow, I think it should be about dead by now. It's been out over three months and I've heard that is the average life of a novel.

Let me hear from you when you get the chance. Looking forward to getting up that way again.

As ever, Mac

To James Oliver Brown, from Route 3, Cordele, January 23, 1955.

Dear Jim:

. . . I didn't get around to mailing this before, and just wanted to add that I think you are perfectly right in what you say about my getting slowed down by other's reactions to any ideas I might want to try. I had been kind of arriving at the same conclusion; and just as John Selby wrote me, if I had suggested to anybody that I might want to write a book about a backwoodsman, or hillbilly, who goes into the army, it would have been turned down in a second. I also know that it is not too good for me to know exactly what I am trying to write anyhow—the best I can do is thrash my way around in the dark for awhile, and maybe see the light toward the end of it. I always thought how fine it would be to be able to try my ideas out on somebody before I went through so much work before finding out whether they would work or not, but I think probably now that was just a mistaken idea. It's hard, though, to get over the idea that there must be some easy way to write, that if you just find the right routine or something, or the right place, there would be nothing to it. But I don't guess there is any sure-fire, easy way, and I would probably do better to go ahead and recognize that fact and quit wasting time hunting, and settle down for the struggle again. If there's not kind of a struggle in it, the book is usually not worth reading anyhow, I don't guess. . . .

Yours, Mac

To Robert N. Linscott, from Route 3, Cordele, January 29, 1955.

Dear Mr. Linscott:

I'm getting kind of worried about all these possibilities of money myself. I'm naturally lazy anyhow and with no pressing reason for doing something about it, I'm afraid of sinking into one of those kind of death-like sleeps that alligators go into. The only thing that might keep me on my toes now is the struggle of trying to hold on to some of it. Already I'm losing friends all over the place—they use to be nice people, but now when they speak to me, I know they are not doing it because they've known me a long time, they're after my MONEY. I'm getting where I don't trust anybody anymore except those who don't like me and won't ever speak to me. Everybody else is a bum, trying to take advantage of me. It makes you right bitter after awhile.

Also, I'm quickly changing all theories of government I ever had. It's one thing to draw the G.I. Bill yourself and try to get by on it while you're trying to get some writing done; it's another thing altogether to think that [some] lousy crum is sitting around school, rooking the goverment, and using my goddamned money. I really resent it; I begrudge them every textbook they get and hope they don't learn anything from it anyhow.

Actually, though, seriously really, I'm mighty glad to get it, but I think I've been wanting to write for too long now to be able to break the habit; and of course, I can't forget how little one book amounts to. I also can't forget, as a matter of fact,

how little all books amount to, probably, but that is something I don't care to think about naturally. That would be
very bad for the digestion and everything else, I'm afraid. I
won't ever go into that very much until I find out I can't write
probably. That's when I'm saving that for.

By the way, my Sister is on the way back to the jungle now
—she's the one who acts; I told you about her; I don't know
whether you remember it or not—anyhow, she has taken a
deep breath and is going to plunge in again, and I have taken
the liberty of asking her to drop by to see you, if you don't
mind. When we were talking about it, you said you knew
some producers and things who might could help her, and if
she could just use your name or something to get past those
dead eye receptionists they have, I know it would be a big
help to her. Would certainly appreciate any suggestions you
could give her.

I have been working when I could on a thing that might be
funny if it works. It was going all right until I saw *Macbeth*
on television; and then I knocked off for awhile to write a lyric
tragedy like that because I got pretty inspired with it, and now
if I keep on with it, I think it has a good chance of being a lot
funnier than the first one I was working on. Will see how it
comes out anyhow. . . .

As ever, Mac

To Max Steele, from Chapel Hill, N.C., March 8, 1955.

Dear Max:
Look, by God, where I am now. I have moved up in the
world, farther north if nothing else, and coincidentally, at just
the place you say you might be at the same time. I had to
finally escape from the jungle down home because too many
details were piling up on me and I was beginning to be chased

down by the Lions and the Elks and others who are always hunting for somebody to speak at them while they digest their food. So I left in the trailer for awhile to try to get some work done, then found this house * which I rented for four months —until June 30—then went back and brought the family up. Just came back this week-end and we are now trying to get settled for awhile. Will probably head back for Georgia at the end of that time, but I think the change might help a little bit. Anyhow, if you do come here in June, the doors are open and we have plenty of room, and I'll see to it that you get some good food, and now I want to buy you at least two drinks because I owe them. I got just as intoxicated over the mighty fine comments you had to make about the novel as I could on a few drinks so I'm due to make it up to you now.

You really don't know how much I appreciate what you had to say. As much as I like the money, I truly don't think there is anything about publishing that makes me any happier than getting favorable comments from people you respect. Your letter to me about the short story gave me more confidence than I deserve to have, and of course, now my ego has gone up quite a few notches. Now I want to write something big and fat and ambitious. It'll probably look like hell, but now I'm really wanting to try it.

As for staying away from the Big Dealers, I think I'm getting an inkling of what you mean, and God knows, I'm trying to keep out of it. I have an agent that I have a lot of confidence in so usually I just leave it all up to him—in fact, I have been doing that so much lately that sometimes I don't know what is going on until I read it in the paper. They made an abridged copy of the book for one place that I didn't even know about until I saw it advertized; and then every once in awhile, he sends me a contract and I sign it and send it back and try to forget about it all again. Of course, he calls me about important things and, as you say, it upsets everything

* At 114 Laurel Hill Road.

when I have to fool with it, so I usually dodge making any decisions about it, and finally have reached the point where I don't give much of a damn what they do with it, play or movie or what-not, as long as they leave me alone and send me the money from it. It's hard to piddle with some little insignificant story when you're having to figure in what is to me outrageous sums of money—I think I'm beginning to see how you could get tied up with something like that. . . .

I'm glad you like old Will. I did too, as I guess was right obvious. I'm going to keep him in the closet for awhile now to be used later maybe in case of emergencies. I cut about eight chapters out of the end of the book * that maybe I can use later if I have to, and there were a few other things I wanted to do with him. He has come in right handy for me. . . . thanks again for the letter.

Mac

To James Oliver Brown, from Chapel Hill, March 16, 1955.

Dear Jim:

I know my reaction to the TV play will be biased, but for what it's worth, I thought I would let you know what I thought of it in case it could be of any use toward making up the play. I wouldn't want you to say anything to anybody concerned about it, except possibly Mr. Evans, because it is all done now and nothing can be done about it, and there is no point in my trying to play the part of a critic unless it might could help some. Anyhow, as a whole, I didn't think much of it—I was pretty disappointed as a matter of fact. Maybe I have no business saying it now being as I didn't say anything when I read the script, but it wasn't until I watched it last

---

* The last fourth of the book concerning maneuvers in Georgia. See letter of April 9, 1954.

night that I felt what I suspected when I first read it, that the whole thing was being played at the completely slap-stick level with a lot of gags and theatrics that really seemed cheap to me. There were a lot of small things that bothered me— probably for that reason, I missed what was good in it, so if I seem overly critical, maybe that's the reason.

Anyhow, even though I like Andy Griffith personally, I thought he over-did everything, trying to play the same kind of character that he did in the FOOTBALL record. Instead of playing Will as a human being who is really serious about all this stuff, as I thought he would, he grimaced and smiled and made faces so that in the end, Will seemed to be nothing but a clown. That disappointed me. I don't myself think Will should be played by a comedian anyhow, particularly one who is trying to be funny. That ruins it for me. He should actually be played just as straight-faced and serious as, say, George Gobels does his stuff. Will is simple but he is also sincere and he shouldn't go around doing gags all the time. It just didn't convince me that way. I can't put my finger on it except to say that he played it on one flat level, that of the moron, which kept it from being believable at all. It looked more like Red Skelton doing his bad little boy act, and it just didn't come through the way I thought it should.

Still, I thought Will showed up better than Ben did. That boy started off hysterical at the beginning and got more so all the way along the line, and when he clapped his hand to his forehead and fainted when he found out he was to be in the Air Force, it made me kind of sick. That was so over-done that it was pitiful, I thought. And the idea of pulling such a gag as he did, "ROTC—Reserved Officers Training . . ." and then blinking his eyes and thinking and then smiling brightly and saying, "Corporation," was a cheap gag at the expense of character. If Ben didn't know anything else, he at least knew the military from the technical point of view, and he would *never* say anything like that. I admit it got a laugh, though—I heard it. Yet I don't think it is worth it to do something like that.

I thought Sgt. King was the best of all, even though I certainly didn't care for that business of his breaking down and crying like that; and I thought the psychiatrist was good up until he put his head down on the table and started crying. There is no point in doing things as unreal as that. You don't have to beat people over the head that way to get a point across. It would have been a damn sight more effective—in that scene for example—if he had just begun looking more and more puzzled, then a little confused, and then fouled-up, and finally, when he realizes what he's done, kind of sheepish and dazed about it. I admit you might not get the quick laugh that way, but if you would just touch it lightly it would be a *deeper* laugh no matter when it came.

I think basically that is what bothered me all the way through it, the fact that it was played at the lowest level, like vaudeville almost, as if the audience didn't have good sense. Take the fight scene for example. That might could have been believable if it had been suggested rather than seen—as it was, it was too quick and impossible looking. I doubt if anybody believed it the way it was. It would have been better, I think, if he had gone into the latrine with them and then the camera would just focus on the door—then you could have a body come flying out every once in a while with a lot of noise going on. Another thing that bothered me right there was the idea of the man coming in to put the notice on the bulletin board and being so completely indifferent to that many bodies laid out on the floor. He wouldn't do that either.

I think the way they managed to move from one scene to the other with Will telling the story was done well. The idea of using a kind of vague background that way seemed to work. Yet I think that once the transition is made from scene to scene with the vagueness, the action and dialogue should be put on a more realistic basis. I could accept changes in scenes that way, but I couldn't accept that same kind of vagueness as far as the characters and actions were concerned.

Another thing that impressed me was that the only things in it that I thought were funny were things that had been written into it, things that Levin* put in and not me. Maybe that was because I was tired of my own stuff or something, but it makes me wonder just the same.

Anyhow, I would like to skim through it and tell you how I felt about parts of it in case it will help with the play. Don't bother to read from here on unless you are interested—it's a dirty trick to sit back and let other people do the work and then step in and criticize it anyhow, I guess. Still, I would like to get it off my chest, and with the hope that Mr. Evans might take a few points I make into consideration, I will go ahead and get it said:

I liked the beginning with the Jew's harp and the introduction into the story except that I thought Griffith over-did it, as he did most of it. I liked the way he got Irvin and the boys into it, but when Ben came in, I didn't care much for that part because I thought Ben was lousy, and I didn't like some of the things he said. He wouldn't say anything about it taking them so long to get a uniform to fit him. Ben was self-conscious about his size and certainly wouldn't advertize it. I've already mentioned the business about the ROTC; I think he would know better than that. The build-up to the fight was all right except that it moved a little too fast—I wasn't ready for it somehow. The fight itself, as I said, wasn't believable at all. In fact, none of that had any sense of being real to me—their quick recovery and following dialogue or the man who came in to post the notice on the board and certainly not that fainting business. Of course, maybe I'm miss-

* Ira Levin wrote the TV script and stage version of the novel. The play is included in *Best American Plays*, edited with an introduction by John Gassner (fourth series; New York, 1958).

ing the whole point in assuming that they meant it to convince, but I still feel that if in the scenes themselves there had been more of an attempt to make it realistic, you wouldn't have to have people clapping their hands on their foreheads, fainting, crying, etc.

The train section was all right, and Sgt. King's beginning was good to me, especially the way he had Will shouting back the "Roger Wilco" stuff. Also, the next scene with Will and Sgt. King was all right except that I didn't like it when he asked which way the Infantry was. I thought the change to the next scene was good, moving into the latrine, and the way he moved straight into the inspection scene. Will shouldn't use a word like "modest," though—I don't know why, though.

What interested me after that was when Will came straight to the camera and explained how nice it had all worked out while far off in the background, you could see the Captain giving Sgt. King hell. This had that kind of double perspective or something that I like to see. It was basically the same kind of thing that Mr. Evans suggested in the first place with the idea of the movie being shown and Will telling the story, so that the audience could see what was actually going on while getting Will's interpretation of it. I wish there were some way to do it all like that.

Most of the classification was all right, I thought, the way they did that, except, as I say, I didn't like the psychiatrist getting hysterical and crying. I liked the way he handled the build-up on the eye business, but I didn't care for the woman officer, even though I suggested that part when I came up there. I suppose on the stage, they can use a Negro officer, though. Also, didn't care for the way Will stood staring at her, like slap-stick again, getting right up in her face that way.

I thought that the next scene in the dining hall when he turned to stare at her again came off well, though, all the way up until the time Sgt. King broke down and started crying. It looks to me as if it could all be handled much lighter than that, with a little more subtlety or something.

Next, the beginning of the plotting against Will, I could see why he felt that Ben should tip Will off, but I wished he hadn't had to do that. Thought the drinking scene was good, especially the lighter fluid—I got a kick out of that, and I enjoyed that scene thoroughly when the fight started with the others, and I thought it was damned funny when Will was trying to talk with Sgt. King as the fellow was choking him. That is not consistent on my part, I know, because I didn't care for things obviously un-real like that in general, but still I liked it for some reason.

The next inspection with the flags and all went off all right, I guess—I thought the funniest part of that, though, was when somebody said, "Watch out for that blasted booby trap." I suppose they'll use the latrine on the stage, though, so there is no need to go into that.

I know all of this sounds very nagging, but it's just the way it hit me, and I think it is probably better to go ahead and say something about it now than wait. Probably it was just that I expected more than that out of it, despite the fact that I have always had a certain amount of doubts about it. I might also say that my reaction does not seem to be typical around here as I have heard a lot of people say they liked it very much. Most of them hadn't read the book, though, I don't think, and were more interested in Andy Griffith than they were Will anyhow—he used to live here, you know. And of course, it's just the opposite with me, and even though I think Griffith did a good job of playing Andy Griffith, I don't think he did much of a job of playing Will—that is, the way I see Will. But maybe all that is natural and I'm just exaggerating it. I hope so anyhow.

I hope all of this has not irritated you too much. As I have said, I don't know anything much about the stage, and maybe I am wrong about it all. I certainly hope so. I'm going to have to make up my mind sooner or later, though, whether I'm going to take part in things like that and assume a responsibility, or keep completely out of it and my mouth shut at the same time. It's not fair to do this way, but I'm taking a chance on it this time in hopes that it might help the play some. I would appreciate it, though, if you keep these opinions of mine to yourself unless you think it might help to let Mr. Evans consider them. I really wouldn't want Levin or Griffith or any of the rest of them to think I disliked their work, whether my opinion would bother them or not. I don't like hurting people's feelings if I can help it—a lot of people I wouldn't mind shooting, but I'm not going to make them feel bad otherwise if I can help it.

By the way, I left the copy of the TV script in Cordele. I'll have to get it from there to send it to you. Received check today from you. Think I have the novelette by the tail now. At least, I'm getting some work done up here. Also piddling around with novel, but I don't know much about it yet.

Will you let me know what you thought of TV? I'd like to know.

Yours, Mac

To James Oliver Brown, from Chapel Hill, May 6, 1955.

Dear Jim:

. . . Leaving in the morning for Calif. It all seems kind of unreal to me. What am I doing, going out to see about a TV show? It's got me confused. Anyhow, I guess it will work out. . . .

Yours, Mac

To James Oliver Brown, from Chapel Hill, May 16, 1955.

Dear Jim:

 . . . I doubt seriously though, if we'll be moving out there [to California]. The more I think about it, the more involved it all becomes. The children need to be settled and when I think of settling, I naturally think of going back to Cordele. I'm going to end up there anyhow, I know, sooner or later, and I just can't see dragging them all over the country because I can't settle down. Probably the best thing to do is settle there and just take trips every once in awhile. . . .

Yours, Mac

To Max Steele, from Route 3, Cordele, July 5, 1955.

Dear Max,

 . . . Things back here, outside of getting settled, are just about the same. Weeds had grown up about two feet high all over the place, and it took a while to get something done about that, and then the well went bad—either we've struck oil or the pump is in bad shape—and I've finally convinced the city that the children will probably be poisoned if they can't run us a water line out that way. So I've done no writing naturally, and from the way things look, it seems that the old routine will hold up for awhile. Around here, there is always something more important to do than writing, something like helping put up a TV antenna or hauling a washing machine out in the country, and I'm a little worried about getting bogged down in it again. But we've decided to go ahead and start building so I might as well get my mind made up to it. It gets on my nerves too, just as you said it did yours, to be in a place where there is nobody to talk to, and as far as building a house goes, I actually don't think I even like houses very much, but we've got to settle somewhere, and this at least gives you a place to get away from every once in awhile. Which is just about what I'm thinking about doing. I'm going to get all this building contracted for so I won't have a thing to do, and then I plan to take off somewhere and hole up for a month or two and go on some kind of writing bender. . . .

You've got me worried over these threatening letters that you received after "Debby." Why haven't I received any threatening letters? It makes me feel like a failure. I've about reached the conclusion that nobody takes my stuff seriously enough to get upset over any of it, and I don't like the thought very much. Next time I intend to write something damned insulting.

I hope you haven't gone and invested your money and found a job yet. That idea gives me the creeps. I think one of the main reasons that I kept writing was that I despised every lousy job I had almost to the extent that I had to do something to get out of it, and writing was my only out. And now to think of somebody who can write *voluntarily* taking a job bothers me. It's probably not as bad when you don't really have to, though. Anyhow, if you are going to invest that money, why don't you invest it down here and we can go in together and drill for oil out where our well is? Might be a fortune in it. That water is thick with oil.

By the way, I hope I didn't give you the wrong impression over what I said about segregation and so on. Even though I don't feel as strongly about it one way as I must have led you to believe in my letter, I don't feel tremendously strong about it the other way either, I don't think. Or maybe it is that I feel very strongly one way for awhile, and then strongly the other way. All in all, though, I'm afraid that I have just never put very much emphasis on it one way or the other. I have seen a lot of individual cases of prejudice that upset me—I can remember one time standing outside a jail for hours while a bunch milled around waiting for them to bring in a negro who had shot the sheriff's finger off, and I was a very happy person when they didn't catch him—but as far as seeing it from any general broad outlook and making any sense of it, I have never been able to. I mean I don't look at OTHELLO as a play of racial prejudice, as I heard a fellow analyze it one time. The fact that he was colored was just a tool as far as I'm concerned. . . .

Yours, Mac

To James Oliver Brown, from Route 3, Cordele, July 28, 1955.

Dear Jim:

. . . I wasn't aware, though, that I was having any more trouble writing than usual until I came to New York the last time when it was brought up to me several times that I was having a lot of trouble getting a second novel done. I don't believe, though, that I'll get stuck on NTFS because I never really put too much stock in it in the first place, and don't care to keep doing the same thing anyhow. . . .

Yours, Mac

To William Blackburn, from New York, September 26, 1955.

Dear Dr. Blackburn,

Just returned last night from a week-end with the Styron's at their place in Conn., which is quite a place. Went up on Friday and came back last night with Ed Hatcher and his wife who had supper with us and were driving back to the city. As a matter of fact, everything lately has seemed like old Duke week. I live only a block from Alec and have seen him quite a bit recently.* My Sister and I had supper with him and his room-mate and some others last Wednesday night, just before Alec's regular classes began. Haven't seen him since so I don't know how it is going with him.

Anyhow, I came up here about two weeks ago with the idea of getting a little writing done, seeing about some things concerning the play and so on, planning to be here for maybe two months, but I don't think I can stick it out. I have changed my plans now and am not going to wait around here for the opening of the play in N.Y., which is on 20th Oct. [at the Alvin Theatre]. Instead, Gwendolyn will come up and then she and I will go up to Boston to see the opening there—then I will go on back to Cordele with her—and hope to God that I can stay put for awhile. For some reason or other, I don't feel at home any place but there—and less so in this god-forsaken city than any place on earth—and always long to get back every time I leave it. I know it is not a good place to write (in Cordele, that is) but there is nothing I can do about it, and I might as well try to accept it that way.

As for the play, everybody seems optimistic. I have not read a script and have only seen one rehersal, which was very rough being as they had not at that time learned their lines, and I personally think that it might have a chance of running for awhile anyhow. It is only a light comedy, a kind of hammed up farce that I personally would probably not pay money to see, but since I have lately become acquainted with some of the plays that are held up to be almost sacred among this legitimate stage loving group and found them to be practically nothing more than B-class movies, with the possible exception of their being able to use the word "damn" every once in awhile—which, I suppose, gives them a sense of being very free in their actions—I have come to the conclusion that NTFS is at least as good as a lot of those. I somehow or other

* My son Alex Blackburn was teaching in a private school in New York.

have a reaction against what seems to me all this worship of the legitimate stage. There is so much phoniness involved that I can't sometimes seperate it from the real thing. It seems to me to be all money—which in itself I don't mind—but I hate to hear them use the word "art" and mean "money." I personally have more respect for the Hollywood attitude—the little I have seen of it—of calling "Money" by its right name and doing so with no shame, than I have of this hypocritic nonsense of talking out of two sides of your mouth at one time. All of which is beside the point, I guess, as I actually do not feel particularly involved in the play except from a financial standpoint. . . . Thanks for the letter. Will let you know how the play comes out.

Mac

To James Oliver Brown, from Route 3, Cordele, October 23, 1955.

Dear Jim:

I didn't get a chance to call you before I left, but I do want you to know how much we appreciate all you have done. So far as I can see, you have been right in every decision you have made—and every decision you have caused me to make (because I actually haven't made any—I only picked out the one you liked best by the tone of your voice or something)—but right or wrong, whether the play turned out to be a success or not, I do want to express my appreciation for all the trouble you have gone to and the interest you have shown and the responsibility that you took on yourself and all the rest of it. This is all badly phrased, I know, and I would rather just buy you a good stiff drink if I were there, but I do want to thank you. I can still remember that if you had not taken over that book and done with it what you did, I would now be working at Warner Robins Air Force Base, and when I think of this, my gratitude knows no bounds. . . .

Yours, Mac

To Max Steele, from Route 3, Cordele, October 23, 1955.

Dear Max,

Your letter was forwarded to me in New York just before I left there to go to see the Boston opening of the play, and since that time, I haven't slowed up much. My wife came up for that, then we came back here—I stayed here a week and then had to go back to the New York opening because my family wanted to go up and they didn't know their way around up there. Anyhow, it is now all over with, thank God, and I am now back down here, as of yesterday, and intend to stay for awhile. The play seems to be all right—all of the reviews were favorable—I have nothing more to do for awhile now except count money, they tell me. I'll believe it when I see it, though. I do feel confident enough financially to go ahead now and see about buying a home, though. We are still living in the one I built before I sold the book, and it is getting too small for us—too small for our heads maybe, but too small just the same. Also have gone hog-wild and bought me a nice boat—when you come down I can take you either water-skiing or duck hunting if you care anything about it. I usually enjoy getting out on the river. . . . I've also had another good break for my morale. The first novel I wrote that has been sitting around in my suitcase for several years now—after I first finished it, I sent it out and they sent it back and I never sent it out again—I finally let them read [it] at the publishing house, and they have offered to publish it if I straighten out the last chapter which is truly terrible.* Also let my agent read it too and he feels that it might do all right, so I might go ahead with it. It is a very morbid book—dead bodies and crazy people all over the place—and I personally don't think I would enjoy reading it much, but, as they say, there is no accounting for taste, and if anybody cares to read stuff like that—I mean when it's *just* that and nothing to lift it—that's their business, I guess. It made me feel pretty good, though, to find out that they think it is publishable, even if I don't go through with it.

Has Chapel Hill changed much for you? I found all of that section changed when I went back—either it or me, probably some of both. I've about given up the idea of trying to find an ideal place to live. Went up to see Bill Styron who lives in Conn. while I was in New York and found it all very pretty, but it only took me a couple of days to know that I would never feel at home there. I know I wouldn't in California either from that trip out there. As a matter of fact, this is about the only place I do feel at home, which is unfortunate because this really is a lousy place sometimes. By the way, I ran into your aunt from Fitzgerald at an eating place here not long ago, and we raked you over the coals pretty thoroughly. . . .

As for New York gossip, I haven't heard much. Styron is working away on his second [third] one now and seems to think it is going all right; I understand Peter Matthiessen has one out [*Partisans*] but I don't know anything about it; also there was a new one at Random House by Irvin Shaw,† but I don't know anything about that either. The Theatre with the capital T seems to me to be the most over-rated hoop-de-do

---

* Truitt Scott hears that his wife Nan has seduced her old beau, Jeffrey Bussey. He kills Bussey, then gives himself up to the sheriff. As if Nan's infidelity had also corrupted their son Paul, a cripple, Truitt sends for the boy to come to his cell and strangles him.

† The *National Union Catalog* does not list a novel by Irwin Shaw in 1955.

I've seen in quite a while. Have never seen more than a few plays and those few weren't much—if they put them in a movie everybody would sneer, but they can put the same damn thing on a stage, and it's supposed to be art. It beats me. They seem to revel in the fact that they can toss off a "damn" or a "hell" every once in a while as if this in itself shows some kind of unlimited freedom. Of course, my glimpse of it was pretty shallow as I saw only one rehersal [of *No Time for Sergeants*], but most of it made me feel that I had rather go on to a movie and relax and enjoy myself. Lots of money, though, so who can gripe?

Let me hear from you when you get the chance.

Yours, Mac

p.s. If this letter is not very coherent, it's because I'm still kind of exhausted. We got in here yesterday and I am still trying to recover from having some thirteen kin folks and friends on my hands in New York. It got to the point sometimes that it seemed they couldn't even eat unless I ordered for them. Really beat me. Never do a thing like that again. This was one time, though, I just couldn't get out of it.

To Robert N. Linscott, from Route 3, Cordele, November 7, 1955.

Dear Mr. Linscott:

. . . Did you hear about everybody getting sued? It's about the scene in the novel, NTFS, where Will rigs up the latrine seats. This fellow had already written up an incident like that and he claims I got it from him. I got it from a fellow I knew in the Air Force, though—he was telling me about a private in the service who was actually supposed to have done that—and I think I can prove it. Have written to the one who told me about it and am expecting to hear this week. Just hope he remembers it.*. . .

As ever, Mac Hyman

To James Oliver Brown, from Cordele, December 17, 1955.

Dear Jim:

. . . Am really enjoying having a decent place to live and a place to work for a change.† I have been fooling around with that first novel and the more I work on it, the more I believe I can make a passable novel out of it. It is not as bad as I remembered it, even though it does make me shudder right often. Mainly, I think, it is a matter of making up my mind of just what I want to do with it. I have to get the main character, Truitt Scott, more clearly in mind, and I also want to get rid of that cheap, smart-alect attitude that keeps cropping up every once in a while. One thing that has helped is that lately I have been reading again, which usually serves to remind me that all books need not necessarily be great monuments of solemn thought that I often in my head imagine them to be. I have read recently Mailer's THE DEER PARK, which, I thought was junk, full of a kind of inverted sentimentalism, which assumes at the beginning that everything is rot, and that is not a bit more true than the assumption that everything is sweetness and light. Anyhow, this kind of thing makes me feel a little better about my own stuff. Also read Peter Matthiessen's PARTISANS which is the first so-called "suspense" book that took me two weeks to dig my way through. I think I like what Herman Wouk says he wants to

---

* He did remember it, and the threatened suit was dropped.

† In late November the Hymans had moved into a large colonial house within the town.

do with writing,* but I don't think he can do it. At least, he hasn't so far, in my estimation. Anyhow, I have been reading, now that I have a place where I can read, and it makes me want to get started again. I read some of these new ones with that blase assumption that the whole universe was manufactured in some little plant over in New Jersey that everybody who reads this or that magazine knows about, and then I turn back to Tolstoy or Dostoyevsky and those old men nearly knock my eyes out. Why can't anybody write like that anymore, I wonder? . . .

Yours, Mac

To James Oliver Brown, from Cordele, March 13, 1956.

Dear Jim:

I have just come back from a week-end in Chapel Hill, N.C. where I have been more or less visiting with Max Steele. I was pretty well bogged down on the novel, unable to make up my mind just what I wanted to do with it, and finally decided to go up and talk with Max about it. Left it with him with the hope that he might see something in it which will clear my mind up on it. It's a long chance—and probably only amounts to stalling—but I thought I would try it just the same. He can get pretty wrapped up in somebody else's stuff and seems to be unable to rest until he gets it straightened out. . . .

Yours, Mac

* This statement probably reflects Hyman's reading of "The Wouk Mutiny." *Time* (September 5, 1955), 48–52. This article stresses Wouk's conservative views on life and literature. A copy of this issue of *Time* is among Hyman's papers.

Linscott had urged the publication of Take Now Thy Son, *in spite of its technical faults, because he was convinced that "Mac is a born novelist and not just a one book fluke." (Memorandum, September 28, 1955, in the files of Random House.) As seen in the following letter, Hyman finally turned down his publisher's offer. The decision was crucial. Just three weeks previously, Hyman had seen clearly "that if I don't go ahead and get rid of it, I won't do anything else." (Letter to Brown, May 2, 1956, in the Columbia University Library.) The confusion arising from a sense of unfinished business was apparent as late as November, 1962: "Sometimes I turn back to the first novel and juggle that around a bit. . . . I have had it for years and cannot make up my mind either to publish it or to throw it away. I think it's a lost cause but I don't have the courage to admit it yet." See Marti Martain, Greenville (N.C.) Reflector, November 17, 1962.*

To Robert N. Linscott, from Cordele, May 25, 1956.

Dear Mr. Linscott:

I was just going to write to you when I received your letter yesterday. I have been holding off to see how things were going to work out and I think now I have finally reached the point where I have to make up my mind one way or the other, and was going to write you about it.

Let me tell you first, though, what I have done. I went back into this novel to the very first, trying to do something else with it, and I guess I must have written the first two chapters some thirty times, trying to make it start out right. None of it suited me, though, so I went up to Chapel Hill for a break, and while I was up there, I had a friend of mine read it as it was. Well, he had about the same opinion of it that you and Jim had, which, it seemed to me, boiled down to the fact that the ending was unbelievable, melodramatic, but that this could be solved by some changes in the last chapter explaining why my hero, Truitt, kills his son. In fact, he convinced me for awhile that this was all that was needed. So I made up my mind to do this. But I still didn't feel right about it so I came back here and started at the first again and re-wrote the whole novel (without making too many changes, though, only shifting scenes around, pointing up this and that, polishing), and got a girl here to start typing on the finished chapters while I worked on the last ones. Through about the first half of it, I got along all right. There was a lot of junk here and there, phony stuff, but time was wasting, and I let it go. And I went along that way right up to the last chapter—in fact, the last three pages of the last chapter—even though I was getting a little sicker by the page, but I kept pushing at it right up to that point. In fact, I even finished it a few times, though I can't be quite sure of this because usually I couldn't read it when I was through. There was something so basically wrong with it that it would make me almost physically sick to look at it. By the time I would reach that point, I could look back and see that the whole thing was unsound and phony, and I couldn't do much about it. The simple fact is that it didn't add up. Two and two make four, and that's all; and I was trying to make out the thing to be more than that. And two and two won't make seven no matter how many times you keep repeating it (which I tried toward the end by summing up a lot of reasons) nor how large you write it (which I also tried.)

Well, anyhow, I went through a good bit of hell with it. You see, I felt the book was phony and I couldn't do anything about it. I don't mean that it is just *bad*. I have written plenty of bad stuff and I have never minded that, but I have never written bad stuff before, *knowing* it was bad. I know I have written a lot of long boring junk, but I have never minded doing that as long as I didn't feel that way about it when I was doing it. If it turned out later that it was junk, that was all right. But to write something phony and feel that it was phony at the same time—that I couldn't stomach. Anyhow, I became very ashamed about it. Sometimes people would stop me on the street and say they were looking forward to my next novel, trying to be pleasant, and I would want to hit them in the teeth. I didn't want them to read my next novel. One night I paced around here and guzzled beer and got the wild idea that it might be all right if I could talk to you and maybe you would then publish it, but wouldn't advertise it or anything. Then nobody would read it and it would be all right. The next day, this seemed a little foolish, though, but then I got the idea in my head that if I published this book, it might hurt my father's feelings because I used a good bit of his background in it. I had thought of this before, but it had never worried me—in fact, I don't know when I have ever been so concerned over somebody else's feelings in something I was writing. But I was and went and asked him if he wanted to read it, to see if there was anything that might bother him, but he said he didn't care anything about reading it, that he wasn't worried, though, so that left me in the same position. I ran out and bought me a few more beers. I know now that I was hoping that he could find something in it that might bother him—then I would have a mighty good excuse not to try to publish it and would feel like a mighty decent fellow besides. This didn't work, though, so I tried to get tough again with it, but ended up getting tanked up on beer again.

Anyhow, what it came down to as I trembled through the next day with asprins, was that I finally made up my mind that I just couldn't go through with it. The way I feel about it now is that even if it were published and then won the Pulitzer and Nobel prizes and then Jesus Christ were to descend and proclaim it the official sequel to the Bible and then even the New Yorker said it was passable, I would still be ashamed of it, and it is just not worth it to me. That might be exaggerated, but it's approximately the way I feel about it anyhow. I don't mind writing junk as long as I know it is junk, and I don't mind trying to write something good and having it turn out to be junk, but I can't tolerate the idea [of] pretending something is one thing when I know it's another. Probably the smart thing to do is polish up these last few pages and send it off to you and let you decide whether or not it can be published, but I still wouldn't feel right about it, and I have never been able to do anything smart anyhow that didn't make me miserable.

Anyhow, I have felt much better since I made up my mind. Went swimming yesterday, feel fine today, and now even feel like working again. I'm sorry for all the trouble it has caused —I know I have taken up a lot of your time with this thing—but there is just nothing much I can do about it. I don't mind now going back into the book and re-doing it from some viewpoint or outlook I could feel comfortable with—something that seemed more like the truth to me—but I think I had better hold off on that for a little while. I don't think my reluctance to leave it this way has anything to do with the fact that it is supposed to be my second novel. I know I won't write one now, or maybe ever, that will have as much luck as NTFS—and I am not particularly worried over how many reviewers upchuck over what I do either; so I don't think that has much to do with it. It's really not one-tenth as important to me whether they like it as it is that I like it. It's my stuff; I'm the one that has to live with it—to anybody else, it's just another book.

Anyhow, we're planning to go to Europe July 5. I hope to leave here sometime around the first and hope that I can get to see you before I leave. As I say, I'm sorry about this, but I know you'll understand how I feel about it. Maybe I can do something better later, even though I'm not going to worry about that anymore. Meanwhile, I am going to rest by working on a baseball story I had. This is only junk but I know it's junk and I think I'll have fun fooling with it.

I hope all of this makes sense. The thing is, I am just

thoroughly ashamed of that book, the way it is. Maybe the reasons I have for being ashamed of it are not the right ones, but nevertheless the fact remains that I am, and until I can see my way clear to doing something with it that is a little more honest, I had rather just drop it. Maybe I should just give up any idea of being a so-called serious writer anyhow.* I do a lot better when I don't take a piece of writing too seriously, when I just have fun with it. I won't go on and on about it, though. I think you probably will know better what I am trying to say than I do anyhow.

Give my regards to everybody.

Yours, Mac

To Robert N. Linscott, from Cordele, June 18, 1956.

Dr. Mr. Linscott,

. . . Have you seen Jim [Brown] lately? Let me tell you what he's gone and done. I think I told you about going out to Hollywood last spring. They paid my expenses and everything to see about doing some scripts for a TV show. Anyhow, I didn't care much about it, but when I got back I wrote this little junky thing and a kind of outline—one page—as to what could follow, and sent it back just to show them that I had given it a try because I felt bad about their paying my expenses and then not going through with the deal. I saw them later in New York and told them I wasn't interested and

---

* From Linscott's reply, June 3, 1956: "No one who can write a letter as sad, perplexed, eloquent, bewildered and amusing as yours of the 25th needs to worry about a career. . . . Note, by the way, that even your frustration and rage are expressed in terms that had me convulsed with laughter. I'd say this means that the good Lord intended you to be, not only a writer, but a humorous one in the tradition of Mark Twain and Ring Lardner. And if you compare your first book with theirs it looks as though you had a chance to beat the old masters at their own game." This letter is in the files at Random House.

thought that was the end of it, but now it seems that Jim has sold them the script that I wrote for a thousand dollars, and the characters too so that they have to pay me a minimum of $250 per week royalties for as long as they televise it. And if it runs into another year, the royalties keep going up. You ever heard of anything like that? All that money for a little piece of junk that it took me one day to write. Of course, I drew on some other stuff I had, but still it seems kind of ridiculous to me. There is also the stipulation that I don't have to write any more scripts for them, so I am under no obligation at all. I've found out now how to make money—you don't have to be a good writer, you just have to have a good agent. I would gladly have *given* them the script just to make up for my expenses that they paid. Anyhow, I think it's pretty amazing.

I am looking forward to getting away from here for awhile. After so long a time, this place does begin to stifle you a little bit. I was thinking about it the other night—of all the people that my wife and I go around with here, I can't think of a man among them who has read a book within, I'd say, the last two or three years. They've read mine but that was mainly through curiosity. Of the wives, maybe two or three have read maybe one or two popular books within the last year or so. And that's no exaggeration. Outside of the librarian and one other person who teaches school (and I don't know him, only *of* him.) I can't think of anybody offhand who would even know who Tolstoy was. This is all right with me, only every once in awhile I want to talk about my business the same way that everybody else talks about his business, but if I ever get started, nobody knows what I'm talking about. They always bring up Mickey Spillane and this gripes hell out of me. So usually I don't say anything about my business. In fact, my best friend here didn't even know I had written a novel until he read in the paper that it was going to be published. Anyhow, as I say, it will be good getting away from it for awhile.

Sometimes I need to hear people talk about books even if it is only a matter of being reminded that they do exist. . . .

Yours, Mac

To Max Steele, from Chapel Hill, September, 1956.

Max:

Been hanging around here off and on all afternoon and finally have to give it up. Where the hell do you hang out? I've checked nearly every place that might make sense.

Anyhow, I found out this morning that Blackburn is down at Pawley's Island, S.C. and being as that is not too far out of the way, I thought I would drop by and see him. To get there before dark, I'll have to go on and leave now. I want to be home on Friday.

Tell Mary Lee* and Diana [Whittinghill] good-bye for me, and how much I enjoyed meeting both of them. Hope we can get together again sometime. I've tried to track them down; finally found Mary Lee's car behind the library, but couldn't find her. She wasn't in the library. Finally figured she might be in one of those trees down by the stadium, but didn't have time to hunt. . . . Let me hear from you.

Mac

To Max Steele, from New York, October, 1956.

Dear Max,

The only reason I was upset about not finding you all the day I left was that I just hated to rush off that way without seeing anybody. Which was why I hunted so hard. And I wouldn't have left so soon except that I thought then, having

---

* Mary Lee Settle, as a Guggenheim Fellow, was reading West Virginia history, the background of her trilogy—*O Beulah Land, Know Nothing, Fight Night on a Sweet Saturday.* She is also the author of two other novels.

some idea of enrolling for classes somewhere, that time was pressing pretty hard and that I had best not lose a day or I might not be able to get off anywhere for this semester. Actually it turned out that I had more time than I thought. After I got back home, I called my agent who got catalogues from both Harvard and Columbia, but being as I couldn't make heads or tails out of them, decided to come on to Columbia because I at least knew the place. Was a little late getting here but have signed up for three classes, and am trying to get started writing now. So far, what with the world series going on, I haven't done much about it, and I have my doubts that the classes are going to work. I have been made to feel slightly self-conscious being in a writing class having already published, and I am a little surprised at how little patience I have left at the usual literary chit-chat and speculation that goes on in those classes. Instead of stimulating me, I'm afraid it kind of depresses me, and already I want to go back home again. I know I'll never last out the entire semester, and am only staying long enough now to get myself back into the habit of writing steadily; and if possible trying to get involved in something that I will be interested in keeping on with. . . .

Did I tell you about the land I bought at home? It's a little over two hundred acres, has three big lime-sinks with fish all in them (I saw a trout in one of them as long as my arm.); it also has doves, quail and duck, and I was pretty happy about running into it. Didn't have time to wait around and check the title so got a deposit on it of five hundred dollars, and now it turns out that the fellow who was selling me the land doesn't even own it. It's all tied up in an estate somehow, and the best I understand now is that it might have to go up for auction. Right now all I'm worried about, though, is my deposit. I have a way of not getting things like that back.

Let me hear when you get the chance. Best to everybody.

Yours, Mac

To James Oliver Brown, from Cordele, November 6, 1956.

Dear Jim,

Would have answered sooner but I have been out of town on a deer hunt for a few days. Didn't get a deer, by the way, even though I certainly thought for awhile there I was going to. They showed me what was supposed to be a deer trail and I followed it and followed it until I found what seemed to me a deer crossing with fresh tracks all over the place; then I hid myself and waited it out for some four or five hours before it finally occurred to me that those might be pig tracks and not deer tracks. It turned out this was right too, but you couldn't shoot the pigs, so after putting in another afternoon of it—this time trying to anticipate which direction the other crowd and their dogs would be driving them—I finally gave it up and settled for a few squirrels, which I never cared anything about shooting. It was a good trip, though, and except for the tent collapsing once in the middle of the night, we had a fine time. Nobody in our crowd ended up with a deer, but in another group, hunting north of us, they killed four. . . .

Yours, Mac

To Max Steele, from Cordele, December 5, 1956.

Dear Max:

I wish you could have made it up for the party.* We really had [a] damn fine time, and there were several people there I wanted to meet you, one being Emmett Rogers, the co-producer with [Maurice] Evans—I wanted to introduce you to him as the original model for Will Stockdale and see if we couldn't work it out somehow for you to try it. Were you really serious about that? I was going to take you at your word

* The producers' party celebrating the completion of the first year's run of the play on Broadway.

anyhow and give it a try—it might have been fun if nothing else.*

Bill Styron and his wife showed up, along with Bob Loomis, and they were all pretty disgusted that you didn't come. The party went on until about five o'clock and even though it was mainly a matter of talking and shaking hands, everybody drank enough so that it seemed to be a big time. G. and I left the next day, Sunday, and went back to Washington, stayed over a night there so I could look around. As many times as I have been through that city, I've never seen anything of it. Styron and his wife were on the way to Baltimore so we rode down that far together. He wants to meet you incidentally—said he would probably be down through that section in the spring and will see you then. . . .

I am trying to get started back to work now, mainly on a war story that I've been piddling around with for several years that hasn't even come close to working out yet. I never could get into the movie script of the Hundredth Centennial for some reason. (By the way, there is a fellow who is wanting to make a ballet of it—can you imagine that? He seemed serious about it, though.) So I worked for awhile trying to make a play out of that junk novelette I wrote, and that didn't work either, so then I went back to the war story again. I think I will keep on with that one for awhile. And I'm going to try to do it here instead of going off and holing up in a room. I never had quite as miserable a time as the last time I was in N.Y.—when you called me there just before I left. The first two days were all right, but then I spent about four holed up in that room, not seeing or speaking to a human being I knew during that time and my work going bad, and I thought before it was over that if I stayed up there another day, I would jump through the window. If writing can't be any more fun than that, I think I would be willing to try to make my living at something else for a change. I'm getting sick and

---

* Steele had once thought of trying out for the role of Will Stockdale in the roadshow company.

tired of agony and I'm not going to put up with it any longer.

Let me know about coming down Xmas. Don't just think about it; make up your mind and let me know.

Thanks again for sending off "The Dove Shoot" [to the *Paris Review*]. Actually, I didn't have too many hopes for it, so I wasn't too disappointed. I don't think I ever will publish that story anyhow.

Let me hear. Yours, Mac

To Max Steele, from Cordele, January 6, 1957.

Dear Max,

. . . Would you be interested in contributing to a book of good first chapters? I think I am going to compile a book out of what I've got here, but might have room for a few others if you've got a terrific start on something but can't or don't want to continue it. I've got a whole mess of them and some of them read right well too. This seems to me to be a good way to get rid of a lot of material. Also you could put those chapters in the public domain and let anybody finish them who might want to. Don't you think that could make a right intriguing book? The more I think about it, the better I like it.

Let me know when you get another telephone. Also about trip to Fla. if interested.

Mac

To Max Steele from Cordele, January 8, 1957.

Dear Max:

To me, that's a damn funny story. I got as tickled at it reading it as I did hearing it even though I already knew about it. Whether or not it could be changed around to a reading, I don't know.* I've been trying to look at it from different angles, and it might could be done the way you suggested, starting it off with the "He did it on purpose idea," even though it would then lose that kind of dead-pan, factual approach that carries a good bit of the humor itself. I wondered whether or not it could be told strictly from a girl's standpoint, switching the parts around, but for some reason it doesn't seem right for a girl's stomach to growl. I mean it's perfectly all right and certainly comic for it to happen to a boy, particularly the way you've done it, but for that to happen to a girl would seem too brutal to be funny. . . .

Wish you could have been with me the other day. We went out to that cornfield in back of Webster's house and had a plenty good shoot. I knocked down about twenty-three that morning (picked up nineteen of them) then went back in the afternoon and got eight more. Everybody out there got almost that many too. That's when they're worth going to. . . .

I have now practically definitely decided to invest whatever money I have left after taxes in land. I've talked to a good many people about it, looked at several different places since you were here but haven't found what I want yet—I think I'm going to jump in with both feet when I do, though. I don't see how you can lose on it. If you buy land that's been cultivated in the last two or three years, you can set it out in pines and the gov. will pay you eight dollars per year rent for each acre you set out—that's what they call rent. Well, if you pay from $50 to $75 per acre (and you shouldn't pay any more than that for pine land) you'll be making, on the average, about twelve per cent on your money—then at the end of, say, twelve years, you should have about a $100 per acre in pine trees, and that's all yours. So in that length of time, you've

* Max Steele, "Ah, Love! Ah, Me!," *Collier's* (November 3, 1945). The plan, never carried out, was for Mitzi Hyman to make a tape-recording of this story, telling it from a girl's point of view.

been drawing damn good interest and you've doubled your money besides. Also, if you have a peanut or cotton allotment, the gov. will pay you about $60.00 per year per acre for *not* planting it. The way I look at it, you can make some damn good money *not* farming. Besides that, I'll be nicking the gov. for some of the money they're getting from me, and that does my heart good indeed.

(Looking this back over—excuse me for running on so. You'll wish you had read more carefully, though, someday when you come down here and find me sitting back with a fortune in pine trees, turpentine spouting out like oil, with nothing more to do than sit and listen to them growing.)

I hope I made you feel miserable about my turning out five pages per day. Have you tried it yet? If you're doubtful, make your students try it—then if it doesn't work, you haven't wasted any of your own time on it. . . .

Yours, Mac

To James Oliver Brown, from Cordele, January 22, 1957.

Dear Jim:

. . . When I'm not writing, nothing much makes sense to me; I lose interest in everything so completely that I don't really care what happens about anything, and am really miserable. I might start thinking about being a farmer, going back into the army, a lot of other things like that, but I don't really care about doing anything. But then when I start facing up to the fact and start writing again, everything changes: I get interested in a lot of things, and if I think about farming or something like that, I can do it with a lot of fun; I start enjoying things again and can't find enough hours in the day to do all the things I would like to do. Even if my work is no good, I am a lot better off, day by day, working on it, than I am when I think about dropping it and trying something else. I've decided that if I can have a good time for a month, it doesn't matter too much really if the work I've done for that month is no good. Because for a month I've enjoyed myself. And furthermore, *all* my work can't be bad. If I can hit it one out of five times, I won't mind too much throwing the other four away. In fact, I'll be glad to throw the other away if I have one good one.

This is the kind of fool logic that I can waste so much time on. I know how obvious all of that sounds, but you would be surprised how long it takes for the most simple things to come clear to me. I'll spend weeks and months coming to the same conclusion that my daughter could reach in two minutes. . . .

Yours, Mac

To James Oliver Brown, from Cordele, March 6, 1957.

Dear Jim:

Styron and Rose came through last Thursday. Spent the night here, then I went with them as far as Jacksonville where he and I took the boat * for a pretty hectic trip down the inland water-way, during the course of which we gave out of gas one time, and ended up being grounded just about dark of the second day. Another boat offered to pull me out that night, nearly got grounded too, then snatched the cleat (or whatever it is) off my boat and rammed a hole into his. Finally the Coast Guard had to come down to show me how to get out. All one hell of a mess. Took the boat back to Daytona myself; my folks met me there to make the trip back

* A cabin cruiser, which Hyman had bought the previous January.

to Jacksonville with me, and I think they enjoyed it. Myself, though, I was worn-out. Got back here last night and am still recuperating. . . .

Yours, Mac

To Max Steele, from Cordele, March 21, 1957.

Dear Max:

I called you awhile back but somebody else answered the phone and said you moved. Just as well, I guess, as that night I had had several beers—that afternoon I had tried playing golf, which I can't do, and that night tried bridge, which I don't know anything about—and just wanted to pester you. Where did you move to anyhow? Why can't you stay in one place for a while? . . .

I'm not doing anything much. The five pages a day finally got the best of me. I got one story off which I understand *Nugget,* one of those pornographic magazines, might take; * and another one off that the Sat. Eve. Post might accept if I cut it down in length. It runs about fifteen thousand words, though, and they want it down to about five thousand. Don't much see how I can do that, though. Have also been working on what was supposed to be another short story but kept going until it got to be about fifty pages and then bogged down on me. Now I don't think I can do much with it. Anyhow, I am getting awfully restless. I have about decided that I am not much cut out for the literary life, and I'm going to write my agent to see if he might could possibly line me up some kind of job in California, movies or TV either one. Don't know whether I can get one or not. I had some offers right after the book came out, when I went out there, but I

* "The Baptism," *Nugget,* II (July, 1957), 6–7, 24, 52, 72.

turned them all down, and now I don't know. I'm going to give it a try, though, anyhow. I'm awfully fed up sitting around, being a reader and a writer and a thinker. I turn out being neither one. I just want to get back to active writing and I don't give a goddamned much what it is. Actually, I like to write, but I'm just smothering to death here. You don't talk with anybody here; you make conversation; and you don't write, you manufacture everything from an audience to a plot. I hate to take the children out of their wholesome, segregated environment, but something's got to be done. And as far as New York, Connecticut, and those place[s] go, from what I have seen of them, have everytime I have been there bored me almost crazy. So I want to go out in the clear bright sunshine and commercialism of Hollywood and join the rat-race. I think I had rather be in the rat-race than no race at all. In fact, I think I'm beginning to like the commercialism. . . .

Let me hear from you when you get the time. I don't talk to anybody around here much. Not long ago I got to arguing with a fellow, and how we got on the subject I don't know, but we got on the subject of living places and I said something to the effect that I had been as satisfied living in a tent as I have in a house, and he went around and told everybody, and now people look at me peculiarly. I did hear what I thought was a pretty good joke a while back though: It seems that some sportswriter was interviewing this lightweight boxer and asked him who his toughest opponent was, and he said Kid Chocoate "because he has this tiny little body and tiny little head."

"Well, how was it you managed to beat him?" the interviewer asked.

"By hitting him on his tiny little body and his tiny little head."

That tickled the hell out of me. I don't know, though. As I say, I'm getting logged around here. . . .

Mac

153 ·

To his wife, from Beverly Hills, California, May 8, 1957.

Dear Hon,

. . . I know that a week or so staying around Cordele doesn't seem to amount to anything; therefore it might be hard for you to realize how hard it is on me to stay in hotels and strange places by myself like this for the same period of time. But it is hard. Every day seems like a week and lonliness makes me almost desperate at times. It's not just a matter of seeing people; I can see Al* and them anytime I want. I could call up Davenport; I could hunt up Aunt Emma's grandson. It's just that I want you all with me. I feel lost without you. So please try to keep that in mind when you're reckoning. A day of waiting here is a long time for me and every one of them amount to something. I know how it is in Cordele when you get so settled into one rut that a week, two weeks, three weeks don't amount to anything much, but I'm telling you when I'm away, I count the hours almost. Half of my time is spent in thinking about when you get here, and I won't be settled until you do. So don't figure time the way it is there; when you start thinking about days and weeks, try to think of it from my standpoint here. I'll never forget the first time I went to N.Y. and got the apartment, and kept calling you, and you couldn't get off because you had to get some clothes cleaned or something like that. I thought I'd go crazy before you got there. And figuring from today, even if you left on the 1st, it would be nearly a month before you get here. And already I have been gone two weeks. So please do what you can. I'll call you toward the end of this week and see if you have been able to work out anything. Let me hear from you, honey. I don't know how to tell you how much I miss you. Kiss the children for me.

I love you, Mac

* Alvin G. Manuel was James Oliver Brown's agent in Hollywood.

Dear Jim,

. . . The play opens out here, I understand, May 22. That is not the New York company, is it? I can't keep it all straight.

I rented this place from a fellow who is a TV writer. Came out here Saturday, glad to get out of the city and the hotel, looking forward to being by myself, and I've had nothing but company since. That afternoon (I got in about noon) a fellow came by and asked me to go to a bullfight down in Mexico. I told him I couldn't make it, but he said he would check with me later. So about nine o'clock, he came back with a friend; they had called off the bullfight and were going to a party instead. I couldn't make that either, so after an hour or so, they left. Then I settled down with a beer, about ready to call it a day, but then this other fellow dropped by. He said he saw the light on and figured I was just sitting around and that he would have a cigarette and keep me company for a few minutes. Well, he kept me company until two-thirty, during which time he smoked about a pack of cigarettes and drank up a good bit of my beer. Sunday was about the same. After fixing my breakfast and settling down to a leisurely cup of coffee, four more boys, two of whom had gone to Duke, dropped in. We talked about people we knew in common; then they offered to drop by on their way swimming to see if I wanted to go. (I think I had mentioned that it was a pretty day.) I said I couldn't make it, but finally went down and had a sandwich with them. Within a couple of hours, it was time for Al and Marianne (sp.?) to come out as we were going to supper. And in between times these little kids kept coming around wanting to know where my children were. "They won't be out here until they get out of school," I told them. So then they would come back every couple of hours wanting to know if they were out of school yet. It was hard to explain. I'm pretty sure they think I was lying.

Anyhow, it's a friendly neighborhood. I've liked most of them I've met. And I feel sure that when it's realized that I don't talk and act all the time like Will Stockdale, things will settle down all right. Usually it works that way. Actually, I enjoy people dropping in anyhow. . . .

Yours, Mac

To Max Steele, from Santa Monica, May 14, 1957.

Dear Max,

 . . . God knows what I'm doing here. As that is my usual reaction to any place I am anyhow, though, I suppose it is nothing to worry about. I came out with the idea of getting down to work, but I find myself now tied up with that goddamned Judy Canova thing again.* This time, though, NBC is talking about doing the producing themselves, and giving me a part of the show if I do a few more scripts. This could mean a hell of a lot of money if it worked as it would be taxable as capital gains, not as income tax, so it is becoming more attractive, junky or not. By the way, would you want a job out here for the summer? If we go ahead with this thing, they will need some more writers, and I think I might have some say-so about it. It's lousy stuff, but there might be money in it, and it should be a way to pass the summer anyhow. If you are interested at all, let me know. As I say, things are uncertain, but it might be worth a try anyhow. Incidentally, I was talking to my agent and I told him that story you wrote about the boy who took the Alka (or Bromo)

---

* Judy Canova had employed Hyman to write a series of TV scripts.

Seltzer, and he's convinced it would make a good TV show.*
Have you ever tried it?

I've rented a house out here about three blocks from the
ocean. It's not too nice a place, but there is a yard for the
children to play, and it will be roomy enough for us. Now I'm
just stalling until the family gets out. I call myself working
every once in awhile. I'm supposed to be putting this script
into script form, but it is so boring that I can stick with it only
a few minutes at a time. I'm beginning to think, though, that
it is not just this that is boring, but all my writing. And not
only my writing, but all writing. I honest to God don't think I
was cut out for this life. I feel that I'm going to pot fast. . . .
I didn't come out here for money, but that is all I can get, it
seems. Not that I have any objection to making it. It's just
that right now it's way down the list of what I need. . . .

Met and had supper with Erskine Caldwell and his wife a
few nights ago. He's a nice fellow. His wife—his fourth—is
about our age and very proud of being Mrs. Erskine. They're
making a movie out of *God's Little Acre* and he was down
here to see about it.

If you're interested at all in the TV thing, let me know
about it. . . .

Yours, Mac

*On the retirement of Robert Linscott, Robert Loomis, now at
Random House, became Hyman's editor.*

To James Oliver Brown, from Santa Monica, May 24, 1957.

Dear Jim,

. . . I always respected Mr. Linscott very much—maybe
even too much for my own good as I nearly always feel in the
presence of somebody who has worked with writers so much

* "Ah, Love! Ah, Me!"

better than I am that there is not much I can add to anything they already know. Why should anyone who has known, say, Faulkner or Hemingway or Thomas Wolfe, etc., truly be interested in anything I have to say or write? This is the way I feel many times, and even though it might be a ridiculous attitude, it is one that is still with me, one that stifles me sometimes. . . .

Yours, Mac

To Max Steele, from Santa Monica, July 8, 1957.

Dear Max:

Sorry I haven't written sooner, but I have been holding off to see if anything was going to come of anything. I did another script which seemed to come out all right, and my agent leads me to believe that people are interested, conferences are going on, wheels are turning, all such things; but so far as I know, things are just where they were when I last wrote you. In fact, I am not doing a damn thing here I couldn't be doing in Cordele, which isn't much. And being as I am tired of all the mysterious happenings which I can't make anything of, I am going to pack up toward the end of this month and head back home. Maybe after I leave they will get more definite about things. It seems that it usually works that way. . . . We spend most of our time going to the beach, or to drive-in movies, and then every once in awhile going out with my agent and his wife to eat. They are gourmets, I think. We discuss food a good bit; then we go out and eat it, and discuss it some more. And being as I usually can't tell the difference between a pork chop and a steak and can't remember from one meal to the next what I have eaten, I am running out of conversation and becoming tired of that too. So as I say, I am going to pack up and head back home.

I do like this country, though, and I like the way the people live. It's one of the prettiest places I have seen in quite awhile and there are plenty of things to do, fishing, swimming, lots of outdoor stuff. And if I could find some way to get those in—if I could find something to do except eat and talk about eating, I wouldn't mind living out here at all.

Not any more news that I can think of. I have been trying to work on a novel, but I don't like it. I have a fine plot, but nothing else. If by any chance you need a plot, I might consider letting you have this one. I can't seem to make it work somehow. Besides, I have finally come to the conclusion that plots only hamper me for some reason. I can't stick to them, and if I try to, I end up with nothing but the plot. No people or anything else. From now on, starting this afternoon, I am not ever again going to write anything but scenes and short stories—then if they grow into a novel, that is fine. . . .

I am thinking maybe if they don't use these scripts as a series that I might try to sell them as separate half hour shows with the stipulation that Sister plays the main role. They'll probably turn them down that way, but I have nothing to lose by trying it except my agent, possibly. He's so hog-wild over the idea of a series I can't even talk anything else to him.

If anything comes up, I'll let you know. I have great doubts that these conference[s] will cease until I leave, though. But then they will. And then I'll hear quite often all that I turned down by just not hanging around another month or so.

Mac

To James Oliver Brown, from Cordele, October 30, 1957.

Dear Jim,

. . . Incidentally, I have been asking about hepititus (It's much easier to ask about than to spell; I have no idea how to spell it.) and the only cases of it I've heard of around here occurred in children under six. This rules out drinking as a causative factor, I think, even though I am not too well acquainted with the children involved. So in case the doctors tell you any different, refer them to me.*

From what I understand about it, though, you're probably going to be in bed for some time. Hope you don't mind it too much.

Things around here are about normal. I am working some on the old novel again. Last night we went to a dance and I became quite loaded and when I saw a fellow standing around holding a hat behind him, I couldn't resist emptying my beer into it and that caused something of a ruckus. He didn't suspect me but he was going to whip everybody at the table so I finally went over and told him I did it to keep from spoiling his night and so we started having quite a few more drinks and tomorrow I am supposed to go out hunting with him on his place. So everything worked out fine. Just hope it works out that fine with you.

Yours, Mac

To Bennett Cerf, from Cordele, February 6, 1958.

Dear Bennett:

Thanks for your letter. Have been meaning to write but I seem to go through the periods when I just don't ever get any writing done.

As for Gwendolyn,† she is now up and around and almost too healthy, so that I tend to forget at times what a close call she did have and become my own mean and hell-raising self again, which is certainly a let-down as I made a good many

---

* In a later letter Brown wrote that his hepatitis was "probably wrongly diagnosed."

† She had almost died of a miscarriage in November, 1957.

vows for awhile there that if she got through it I would never again stoop to such things as complaining about the children making too much noise, the food being too salty or not salty enough (according to my disposition at the moment)—in fact, that I would never again do anything to disturb, upset or irritate anybody at anytime. But, as I say, she is now healthy again; and I have again allowed my disposition to lapse right back down to its humdrum average level.

I am now trying to get in four hours of work per day except on Sundays which I used to good effect by figiting around all day learning all over again that compared to figiting around, work is not so bad after all. I do hope something comes of it soon. One thing that keeps me going is a remark you made the morning after that play, NTFS, opened in New York. I doubt if you remember it, but you told me about going to the opening of MISTER ROBERTS with Sinclair Lewis,* and of his saying that nothing worse could have happened to Thomas Heggen. I don't mean that the way it might sound— I don't mean that the success of the novel or the play either has made me the least bit unhappy (I am not that insane)— but I do mean that at times, when desperation was ready to set in, I have been able to stall it for awhile.

Give my regards to your family and everybody. G. sends hers along too.

As ever, Mac

Hyman wrote this account of No Time for Sergeants *at the request of Warner Brothers, who produced the movie version of the book. In a letter dated May 22, 1958 (now in the Columbia University Library), he enclosed the following copy for James Oliver Brown.*

* In February, 1948, at the Alvin Theatre in New York. Thomas Heggen committed suicide on May 19, 1949, for reasons which are still obscure.

The other day I received a letter from a German student asking me my reason for using the quotation: "This is definitely a violation of regulations"—the comment made by General Mark Clark on the prisoner uprisings in Korea—at the beginning of the novel *No Time For Sergeants*. He had the feeling, he wrote, that this plays an important role for a serious interpretation of the book.

Aside from the fact that this was a *very* serious student (so much so, in fact, that he was also making a study from the linguists point of view and had just completed counting the various "anyhows" and "sos" used), and aside from the fact that it was downright flattering to me to be taken seriously about anything at anytime by anybody, I was particularly glad to answer his letter in detail as I could truly answer that the General's remark did have some meaning for me—in fact, a kind of double meaning. One of these was purely personal and had nothing much to do with the novel at all for I was, when I wrote that book, myself violating some kind of regulations that I had somehow set up for myself in writing. I don't know how to explain this except to say that I had been trying to write for a long time and had been writing—with no success—what I thought of as serious and possibly even literary stuff. I had also tried to keep in mind various notions (vague as they were) that I didn't even know I knew, things that I had been told about writing, things that I had read, etc. —most of which had far more to do with how not to write a bad novel than how to write a good one.

Anyhow, these notions were, I finally discovered, hampering me a good bit. Therefore, when I did this one, I decided I would just enjoy myself; I would violate all those notions—no matter how profoundly they had been stated and no matter how omniscient the critic or reviewer seemed—and write it the way I felt it ought to go. This gave me a lot more freedom and fun than I had had with writing for a long time. I found it suddenly unnecessary to write about what seemed to be the burning topics of that time—such things as Liberal thought, homosexuality, anti-Semitism, horrors of war, and so on, such issues that absolutely had to be included in a novel for it to be considered "serious" (This was of course a few years back—by now of course the fashionable issues have changed.)—and I could write about what interested me. I think up until that time I had the feeling that it was somehow wrong to write comedy about what might be thought of as serious, that I would be quickly put in my place for not having assumed the properly morbid attitude, full of defeat and dispair, weeping futilely in the darkness and so on—so it was a violation of something or other. Maybe this was because I was in Houston, Texas at the time, but I was not particularly excited over what were supposed to be the real issues of the day, and as for the general and seemingly accepted attitude that young men had emerged from World War II as bitter and disillusioned, I myself didn't feel that way at all, and I didn't see many people who did. As for myself, I was just very glad to be alive and curious as to what would now happen to me. I didn't expect to save the world or democracy or anything else when I went into it, and I think I had a fairly good notion of what war was like; in fact, to be honest, I don't think I saw all during World War II anything about war which particularly shocked or surprised me.

Anyhow, that was part of it, the personal part. The other thing I meant to convey, which has more to do with the novel, was that basically, from a certain point of view, there is nothing much that man does, no matter how serious it seems at the time, that is not also slightly ridiculous. There is nothing original about this thought of course, but certainly Mark Clark's comment, stated blandly, was, when you stop to think of such an unlikely situation as having a group of prisoners in a camp rebel, capture the officers in charge, and hold them as hostage (which actually happened) a kind of unbelievable, almost farcical situation. The General's foolish observation—

"This is definitely a violation of regulations"—repeated flatly on the front page of many papers at the time, almost as if it were a news scoop, at the height of this crisis, struck me as almost the limit of absurdity; and as I considered the Korean War as something farcical, [a] comedy of errors anyhow, I couldn't help but be fascinated by it.

I don't mean by this that I sat around giggling over the whole mess. As a matter of fact, I was pretty much upset and confused by it all. I was back in the Air Force at the time and one of my jobs was to call on and help straighten out insurance, back pay, etc. with the families—parents and wives—of some of the men being killed. This was certainly not amusing to me. Neither was the incongruity of the fact that during this time also I received letters from friends of mine in New York every once in awhile during this period and found almost all of them nearly unaware of the war but vitally concerned at the time over whether or not Mr. Hiss might have to spend a few months in jail. As I had some thirty casualty cases at the time, some of them the families of men I had known and more coming in every week, I was not too concerned with Mr. Hiss and could not truly visualize how anybody else could be. But when I wrote back and inquired as to what they thought of the progress of our new war, I got back other letters, most of them upholding it in principle and pointing out very logical political reasons for it. I did not put too much stock in these letters, though, as I personally knew of no one who—because he strongly approved of what was going on in Korea—went right out and enlisted again. Instead, I saw men who had been in and didn't want to be in again, re-called, given six-week refresher courses and sent out again. And at the same time I was feeling very guilty about sitting around an Air Base in Texas with a desk job, and also something of an idiot for even considering that there was any point in trying to go over and fly another tour in Korea.

So I did not find the Korean situation a laughing matter—

far from it. But there comes a time, it seems, when a man has almost got to laugh to preserve his sanity. Perhaps this seems to be making more out of it than the material warrants (in fact I know it is because I know what I cut), but in the back of my head and inside me this feeling was there most of the time, and for a change I listened to it.

As for the language used, as I told the German student, I don't know a lot of times why I used "anyhow" and "so" except for pace and such things. If they felt right I left them there. Actually I did not think of this novel as being in dialect until several publishers had turned it down on the basis that it was in dialect, and they had rules too, one of which that novels in dialect would not be read anymore.

Anyhow, I appreciated the letter from the German student, and I enjoyed answering it. It is certainly flattering to be taken seriously sometimes, particularly when you are not sure yourself of just how serious you are.

To James Oliver Brown, from Cordele, July 8, 1958.

Dear Jim,

Sorry I haven't written sooner but have recently in my downright desperate state of wanting something to do been traveling all over the southeast trying to find some kind of newspaper job. My wife's mother came and got the children and took them to Florida for awhile, and Gwendolyn and I took off first for New Orleans where we spent a few days while I went around talking with various editors without much success. I think part of the lack of success (and just part of it too because I realize I know nothing about the newspaper business) stemmed from the fact that most of them thought I was slightly batty. At least, that was my impression, particularly when they would come right out and ask me, and also when they would go off in corners and whisper to each other about it. Usually after that it came down more to myself convincing them that I was in my right mind than it did in discussing any kind of job. And this usually relieved them, it seemed; we then shook hands and said how glad we were to meet each other, and that was it. I have begun to think since then that a good bit of it too was that I probably didn't really want the job in the first place. God knows what I would have done if they had actually made some kind of proposition.

But I did try two newspapers there and in between time had a fairly nice time wandering around New Orleans, which I like very much with the exception of their so-called famous eating house, Antoines, where we got a couple of Howard Johnson steaks that were disappointing. Also had supper one night with Harnett Kane,* whom I had met here in Georgia, and enjoyed that part of it anyhow.

By that time, though, I had run out of money so instead of going directly to Florida as I had figured, had to come back through Cordele to go to the bank, then left the next day for a couple of days at Daytona, and then on down to Miami where I started on the newspaper business again. The children were at Fort Lauderdale, just north of Miami, so we moved to a motel there for a few days while I went back and forth. Checked with the Miami *Herald*, convinced the girl at the desk that I wasn't going to fill out any damned application blank (I've filled out enough of those things in my life); convinced then in turn the personell director, managing editor, and city editor that I was sane, and finally even covered a story for them. Very interesting story about a man who had tried to divorce his wife ten times, succeeded three times but each time re-married her, finally—about five years ago—killed her and left her floating nude in a canal (they could never prove this, but it seemed fairly obvious); then the night before had finally killed himself. But with all the who, what,

* Journalist and author who lives in New Orleans.

where's and when's, and not being able to say what you knew, I did a very lousy job of it; and finally decided I didn't care anything about this kind of work anyhow—instead I would try a couple of feature articles and see how they went.

So over the week-end and I gathered material and didn't have to look much further than the motel where we were staying because they had there one of these coppertoned swimming instructors who damned near drowned a boy right in front of my eyes while the boys father sat there and chortled and the mother kept hopping up and taking pictures of the boy with her little Brownie camera as he clung to the bank and pleaded to be let alone, gurgling up water most of the time. But I made a mess of this one too as I was too full of downright malice and was mainly interested, I think, in getting old Coppertone fired and the parents turned over to the authorities for cruelty to children. So there was nothing particularly humorous about it—nor about the other one that I tried, which isn't even worth mentioning.

Anyhow, then I decided to come on back to Cordele, feeling actually a hell of a lot better having got the newspaper bug out of my system and realizing I didn't really want to do that. What I want to do is to write novels. And that's all. . . .

By the way, we had the grand southern premiere of the movie here on July 3, and I would say about forty showed up for it, outside of my family—and as the old joke goes, some of them found it so funny they could hardly keep from laughing. Frankly, I kind of enjoyed it, though. . . .

Yours, Mac

In an experimental mood, Hyman decided to enter the Walter F. George School of Law, Mercer University, Macon, in September. "I kind of resent the idea that because I wrote a novel one time, I am automatically incapable of doing any-thing else." (*Letter to James Oliver Brown, October 8, 1958, in the Columbia University Library.*) *He tried to keep this new interest quiet, however, telling the local newspaper that he would prefer not having his decision mentioned. That evening, it was mentioned in a newscast from Macon. He dropped the study of law officially in November.*

To Max Steele, from Cordele, fall, 1958.

Dear Max,

. . . Have been right busy with the law school even though some SOB up there called the newspapers and made a big deal out of it, saying I was going to be a lawyer and what-not, so that it almost ruined the whole thing for me. Newspapers kept calling—thinking, I guess, that they had some kind of human interest story—and I was asked several different times if I would mind stacking up a bunch of books and staggering across the campus looking like a fool so that they could take pictures of it. I finally got right mean about it, made quite a few enemies by refusing to go through with the foolishness, and became downright snappish about answering questions. It was miserable, though. Even Time magazine called. I've never been made to feel like such a freak in my life.

So even though I was enjoying the classes, all the rest of it was about ruined for me, and I was hunting for a good graceful out when one presented itself to me. They called from California and said they were ready to go ahead with the pilot film on the TV thing and would I come out there for about two weeks? Decided I would and am leaving tomorrow, flying out, as much as I dread it. I couldn't very well turn it down, though. This is all I will have to do with it, and if the thing goes over, there will be a hell of a lot of money involved. I won't have to write another script or anything unless I want to myself. So I guess I am on my way.

Had somewhat trouble with that too, though. Some TV gossip writer on the Atlanta *Journal* picked up this information from a Screen Gems publication, and went on to make a kind of snide remark about this series being an imitation of another series called *The Real Mccoys*—a new popular one, I guess—which I haven't yet seen. This made me so mad that I was sick for a couple of days. I called him up and told him just what I thought of him, wrote a letter roasting him, got the *Journal* to agree to run it; then I waved it over his head—figuratively speaking—until he agreed to retract everything, which he finally did. I really chewed him out, though. His voice was quavering before it was over with. He damn well had it coming, though. On the phone he claimed he didn't mean to imply that *I* had imitated anybody; the way he understood it—he said—was that the screen company had set the thing up and that I was just going to work on it.

Anyhow, I have been going through hell and think I am on the verge of a nervous breakdown. A few more months of this kind of desperation and I will be. But I'm going on out to California for a couple of weeks, get through that, and if I don't get killed on the airplane—which I always expect—I'm going to make some changes, all the way around. I'm through being doctor, lawyer, Indian-chief—or anything else that comes along. I'm mighty tired of spending my life in other people's back yards. I'm going to retire completely from all troubles everywhere.

I would send you along the boat story,* but the only copy I have here is the one without the cuts in it, and now that I have seen how effective the cuts were, I'm ashamed to show it that way. But I'll make the cuts in this one and send it as soon as I get back from Calif. if you're still interested. . . .

Mac

* "Vital Tips from a Boatman," *Esquire*, LI (February, 1959), 100-10.

To William Blackburn, from Cordele, November 24, 1958.

Dear Dr. Blackburn,

Congratulations and many thanks for the book.* It came in the other day when I was in the middle of something else, but naturally I was interested in looking through it, and ended up dropping the other project completely which was of shallow interest compared to yours. I don't have much of a scholarly mind, I know—I guess about the only yardstick I use on something is whether or not I can use it myself, whether or not I can learn something practical from it, but from that standpoint I think [I] gathered something. But what are obvious to many people are miracles of discovery with me, and I am always fascinated with the purely physical circumstances that help to bring about good writing, and of course these letters bring that right to your mind immediately. It was really exciting to me to have a picture of this sort of Conrad really working—not only at his writing but at all the other things a writer has to put up with in order to turn out his stuff. Take for example this business of the relationship of a writer with his audience. Always I wonder about that when I read a good book because any writer any good has to have a good reader somewhere, I think. Hemingway had Gertrude Stein, Faulkner that Mississippi lawyer, Shakespeare his regular audience which must have been a terrific one—anyhow, here I find one of Conrad's audiences, and again it confirms in me that absolute necessity of having a good one. They obviously expected good work out of Conrad and that's what they got. They could certainly have gotten something less if they had wanted and expected no more.

Also, this business of Why a Writer Writes—and I am not talking about those deep so-called subconscious motives, etc., whose existance I sometimes doubt completely, but just those purely practical—even common or vulgar—incentives. I don't

---

* Joseph Conrad, *Letters to William Blackwood and David S. Meldrum,* ed. William Blackburn (Durham, 1958).

feel that either the psychiatrist or the preacher can give a satisfactory explanation on their own level; so I don't even question the Why anymore—just accept the fact that the drive does exist. But those practical incentives—those mean little things that actually get the work done—those can be studied, and something useful can be learned from them. It's real to me to see Conrad struggling with his debts. How wonderful it is, it seems to me, that he wasn't a rich man. He had to keep writing to keep living, once he got started with it. Of course, once this incentive was lost, he could have invented another one, (and probably would have had to as no man lives in the clouds all day) but that too is interesting.

But I won't argue the point. What I am trying to say is that I think this is a damn fine book and I have enjoyed it. It is not the answers I get from it anyhow that prove its worth; it is the fact that it does raise those questions that give it excitement.

I have been to hell and back this past year; will not go into details right now as I still haven't emerged and it is too depressing to go through again. Will write later when things are clearer, assuming that they will someday get that way.

Thanks again for the book. I am mighty proud of it and know you must be too.

As ever, Mac

To Max Steele, from Cordele, December 1, 1958.

Dear Max,

I agree with you right down the line that I ought not to be piddling around with such things as law, and that I ought to be writing novels or something like that. (Only nothing quite so trite as Tolstoy; * today I feel much more ambitious than

* In an earlier letter to Hyman, Steele had praised the scenes of country life in Anna Karenina.

that—I have my ups and downs for a fact.) Anyhow, with that in mind I have now resigned from the law school and am now spending my time pacing the floors and raging because I am bored and not doing anything. But I do have something in mind and this time the whole goal will be in writing and nothing else. What got me onto it was that trip out to Hollywood. They gave me an office so I could get up in the morning, drive to work, have somebody to show my work to, then leave. Doing this, I had the rather fantastic (to me) luck of writing detailed outlines for three scripts in one afternoon, and another the next day—none of them bad either as far as TV scripts go. This is more work than I had done in the previous six months and it came to me very clearly then what I had to do. If I stayed around the law school, I would be wrapped up in the law; if I quit that and stayed around Cordele I would spend all my time following the football team (which was a good one this year) or hunting and other such things; if I stayed out in California, I would end up interested in TV and movies—it's all according to where I am and what is going on. I looked back on everything I had ever done in writing and in other things, and this seemed to me to be consistent. So I decided that being as I am really more interested in novel writing than anything else that the only thing to do would be to go to where the novel writing is done. Which is, goddamnit, N.Y. which I despise but don't seem to be able to avoid. Anyhow, I am going to write to them [Random House] today and ask them if they could find me a place to work around there. . . . Then if I had somebody to read my stuff, I could write some novels. In fact, being in those circumstances, I don't think I could help but write some novels. It would be a natural thing, and I would not then feel that I live in this strange, unnatural world of mystic art that is so isolated and lonesome to me.

So that is what I am now planning. I hate to have to move

the family out of here, but I have no choice. It's true I ought to be writing; everything else is only a substitute, and God knows I am tired of it. . . .

No news around here much. I think the TV thing will go through all right (even though I lose interest in it as soon as I leave there) and I stand to make a good bit of money from it. I have a kind of unbelievable deal with it—can turn down any actor, director, script etc. Get paid for the use of the characters and the format, as they call it; an extra $2000 everytime I write a script; $250 per week extra even if I don't write a script simply for being a consultant; royalties and part of the profit too. Of course, all that is meaningless unless the thing is a hit. Then it will amount to nothing. (Incidentally, I know the secret of how to get along out there: Don't give a damn. Then they're dying to get you. And you don't even have to say anything—all you have to do when things are not going to your liking is tell them that you're going home. It works everytime.) . . . Let me hear.

Yours, Mac

To Robert D. Loomis, from Cordele, December 1, 1958.

Dear Bob,

Listen, don't *ever* worry about prodding me. There's nothing on God's earth that I need more. I can look back over everything I have ever done—which amounts now to so miserably little—and each time it has been a matter of writing something because somebody has been interested in reading it. This is always true—all the way from Blackburn's class, to TV scripts, to short stories or anything else. And just the reverse is true too. When nobody is interested in hearing a story, you don't tell a story. And also you almost automatically tell the kind of story that somebody wants to hear. No writer is any better than his audience and he can be good only with a good audience and he'll do nothing when he has no audience. This I know about myself for a fact, and I suspect it all the time in other writers too. When Faulkner wrote for newspapers, his stuff was no better than other people writing for newspapers; when he wrote for that lawyer in Oxford or for Sherwood Anderson or Saxe Cummings, it was a different thing. Same is true with Hemingway, Wolfe, and I would even think Shakespeare too. You could never bother me by prodding me—just the opposite. I am so flattered when somebody wants me to write something, wants to hear a story from me, that I will work like a mad-man. Not long ago out in California in one afternoon I did detailed outlines for three TV scripts (and I don't even like TV scripts) and they weren't bad for TV scripts, simply because somebody was interested enough, because somebody wanted to see what I could do. Did a fourth the next morning too. This has been true all my life. Reason I wrote for Blackburn was that he seemed interested. Same was true up at Columbia too. I did more work there in three months for Selby and Helen Hull than I had done in the previous three years. Man, I *hunt* for audiences all the time; nothing can quite set me off than having somebody wanting to see something (Hell, you ought to know this. I never would have put the first few chapters of NTFS together if you hadn't written me and asked me if I had the beginnings of a novel.)* That and the competition—truly I thrive on the competition; it brings out the best and meanest in me. . . .

As a matter of fact, I'll make a bet with you. You can name

* "It was Bob [Loomis] who first caused me to start putting No Time for Sergeants into book form. He wrote to me when I was in the Air Force, asked if I had anything—this set me off trying to make a few chapters out of the short sketches I had made." (Letter to Bennett Cerf, May 22, 1957, in the files of Random House.)

the amount yourself. You find me some small cubby-hole of a room up there at Random House (a place to work—I hate working around the house; I like to get up every morning and go to work like everybody else. This seems normal and natural to me; I think you pointed out to me one time that I felt guilty about being a writer, and I think you're right, and I think this takes some of the curse off it.)—anyhow, you find me just any kind of place to work and agree to look at my stuff every couple of days or so—whatever I have turned out during that time—and I'll bet I can have a novel that you wouldn't be ashamed of publishing by June of next year. Will work five days per week on it. I'll move the whole family up there somewhere, rent a house, and commute. I think I can do it, and I don't say this with any bravado—I simply believe it and am willing to gamble the time and effort.

The reason I say I need a place to work (like at Random House) is that I truly *need* to see people interested in books. Makes it seem a normal way to make a living or something. I know, for example, that I care nothing about TV scripts, but if I get out there and actually *see* people interested in the things, I'll start trying to turn them out too. And so far I've had good luck with that kind of work. Only it is never really satisfactory because what I really want to write are novels that are sound and solid and can be stacked up on a shelf. But I am going to work at whatever is around me to be worked at (be it law or shotgun shooting—I've dropped the law, by the way; have become a right good shot, though.) and it might as well be novels as I like them better anyhow.

I'm not kidding. All this is not as haphazard as it sounds. I've thought about it hard and long. If you're willing to gamble some of your time, I'm willing to gamble nearly all of mine. . . . Let me know when you have the chance.

Yours, Mac

To Diane Wright, from Cordele, January 7, 1959.

To Miss Diane Wright and Newton County High School: *
. . . If I seem to be taking this lightly, it is only because I
mean to. For even though it might be pleasant to have attractive features, this is by no means the end-all and be-all. Some
of the handsomest people are also some of the unhappiest; and
looks anyhow are a matter of taste. I have never seen a girl who
wasn't pretty one way or another. But again I would like to
say all this is relative. Who, for example, is more handsome:
Sal Mineo or Abraham Lincoln?
I would like to congratulate all of you for finally reaching
the stage of graduation. And I hope that each of you—after
some eighteen years of rest and recreation—is now willing to
get down to work for a change.
Congratulations! May each of you get what you want out
of life; and still want it after you've gotten it.

Sincerely Yours, Mac Hyman

To James Oliver Brown, from Cordele, February 4, 1959.

Dear Jim,
. . . We went down to Sarasota first, with the idea of
moving down there maybe. Looked at houses a couple of days,
checked up on all those necessary details like schools, etc.,
looked at houses from all kinds of practical standpoints—both
rental and for sale—spoke very logically of all the advantages
a place like that has over a place like this, moped around for
two or three days seeing the quiet, nice places and the retired
people and the very obvious artists with their beards and those
charming places with the views (as if anybody can look at a

---

* Hyman and his wife had been asked to select from small photographs the
prettiest girls and the handsomest boys in the Newton County High School,
Covington, Georgia. His letter, from which this excerpt is taken, appeared in
the school annual for 1959.

view for more than five minutes without getting bored)—
then finally said to hell with it: I didn't like the Gulf anyhow,
and didn't care to tie up a lot of money in a city where I felt
out of place.

So we took out of there, went by to visit a friend of mine in
Leesburg, Florida, and then decided to go back by way of
Daytona Beach, as that is one place that I have always liked.

So we spent the night over there and on the way out the
next morning, saw a place I liked very much right on the
ocean, stopped and found out about it, and ended up buying
the damned thing—fifty thousand dollars worth. But now, by
God, I'm glad I did it. . . .

Yours, Mac

To his sister Dinah, from Cordele, February 5, 1959.

Dear Dinah,

Last night Gwendolyn and I were talking and we both had
what I think is a good idea if we can get you to do us a favor.
Mama said she called you about the house we bought down at
Daytona—what I had in mind was this: I don't like the colors
of the walls and G. doesn't either, particularly in the living
room which is now some kind of dark, purple color. Well,
what we were thinking we would ask you to do is maybe go in
there with some paint some week-end and do a large mural of
some sort on it—the whole wall. I had in mind just a kind of
jungle setting, very bright (G. said with a lot of pinks, etc.)
and loud, just an impression or something with trees, flowers,
splotches of them all over the place. Would you be interested
in giving it a try? . . .

Mama told me about Dan Standard's idea,* which sounds
to me like a good one. At least, it can be a good one if you

---

* That is, to supply his interior decorator's shop with a number of her
canvases.

don't take it too seriously and tighten up on your painting. I don't mean to set myself up as an authority on painting, but I do know from experience that most creative work demands something of the same conditions, and these are only practical matters which I have found very useful. And what I say about taking a certain piece of work—any kind—too seriously and tightening up on it so that you don't have the same easy freedom of movement and feeling and thought is the same for all. That is basically, I think, the difference between an amateur and a professional. The main thing that a professional can do (and this is in sports, writing, painting, etc.) is to discipline himself so that he still controls the work instead of the work controlling him. That is important. From my own experience, I know that I have always had the best luck when I was trying the least. I didn't work hard or seriously on NTFS, The 100th Cent., The Dove Shoot—and several others that came out all right for me. I did them for fun, for enjoyment. On the other hand, I have maybe thirty different stories, pieces of novels, etc., that I worked hard and seriously on —they have never come to life and never will. And this is true of most work that is creative. For example, Al Manuel, my agent, was worried with me because I did not take the TV series seriously, until it finally occurred to me (and as I told him) I could not even write the things if I took them seriously.

I use my own stuff as an example only because I know it best. I could quote probably fifty cases of the same attitude, though, because I have seen it work enough. The same is true of Faulkner in his earlier and best work—he said himself about *The Sound and the Fury* that it was never work because he was having so much fun doing it. And he told me *—and it makes sense—that unless you enjoy what you are writing, there is absolutely no point in doing it. As I say, I could cite quite a number of cases like this: the ultimate case, though, I

* Hyman had met Faulkner at lunch on Robert Linscott's invitation.

would think, would be Shakespeare who seemed to have no more reverence for the stage than any hack writer would have for TV. He was mainly interested in making money, and this gave him a range of writing impossible for most modern day writers who go into such things as capital A "Art" as if it is the end-all and be-all. Shakespeare knew better; therefore he had the poise of a real artist, not the drive and determination of a hack. (Not that he didn't work hard—he did, but never desperately, it seems.) Also, Tolstoy wrote *War and Peace* that same way, as hard as it might be to believe when you read it. But he did. He wrote it mainly for fun, for entertainment —it was not until he was practically through with it that he began taking it seriously at all.

What I am trying to say is that you must set up a system of values in which you are controlling the work. That means you've got to enjoy it; if you don't, it won't be any good anyhow. I don't want to belittle Dan's business proposition but I think you should [be true?] to yourself. Don't let it make you desperate or serious. It doesn't amount to that much. You always have to keep a light touch. And this has nothing whatsoever to do with whether material is *serious* or not. Comedy and tragedy work the same in this respect. Don't allow hopes of money or another job [to] spoil your natural enjoyment of your painting. It would be better not to have money or change jobs—your work will be better that way. Hemingway said one time, "Anybody who tries to write an epic, writes a bad book." I would imagine the same would be true in painting or anything else. You try too hard to do something and it gets to the point that you are tired of it, bored with it, and it shows in the work. And the one unforgivable thing about a book or anything like that is for it to be dull and boring. Any kind of art should be alive and you don't get that with a worried desperation, a sick kind of ambition, but by an almost indifferent joyful attitude, as if you really don't give a damn. (Which is, truly, the only reason I have really ever made any money—simply because I didn't give too much of a damn whether I did or not.) . . .

Love, Boy

To James Oliver Brown, from Cordele, April 23, 1959.

Dear Jim:

. . . Really, you have never seen such a mess as had been made out of it.* It was not any terrific piece of writing in the first place, but at least it moved along with a little pace, the characters—though caricatures—were somewhat believable, and even though it was mainly slapstick stuff, there was a little bit of room for your imagination to move around in. But now it is absolutely nothing. It is slow, dull—everything spelled out and clear—the characters are so unreal that nobody could ever believe them; they have so little dignity that it is not funny when they lose what little bit they are supposed to have; it is now a collection of Milton Berle wisecracks in which the characters themselves seem to think that they are funny, which is, as far as I'm concerned, killing to any sort of comedy. Worst of all, though, is the dialogue. I have never seen anything to equal it. It is so strained that it is downright painful; the writer goes at it with the idea, it seems, that backwoods people always speak in long, ridiculous similies the way they might in comic pages, and he makes up one right after the other to prove it. And when I say "makes up", I mean it. Certainly, he has never heard talk as this anywhere in his life. Listen to some of these: "You bleat like a wounded hoe handle." "I can summon up a right feathery hoot owl." "I know you can shoot the hop right out of a cricket." "There's more of them around than a razorback's got bristles." "With

* Others had rewritten Hyman's original TV script.

the speed of a hawk, we'll descend on them." (That one is the army talking.) "Outlanders!" "You'll be finding your head in a wagonload of punkins." "He's got about as much gumption of a helpin' of red ham gravy." "She loved it here 'cause God lifted these hills so close to Heaven that children could just reach up and tickle the feet of Angels." (I had to step into the other room for a few minutes after that one.) "I'll be tromped on a toadstool!" "Hand me my old trusty." (In all my life, except in a joke, I have never heard anybody refer to his gun as a trusty.) "They won't just laggledag around." "You've got to stop this fractioning." (God knows what that is supposed to mean. Not "fractious"; it is not even used in that sense.)

I could go on like that for quite awhile, but it's pointless, I guess. Actually, the thing is so horrible to me that [it] fascinates me somehow. When I get that tired feeling, I can use it instead of Geritol. I can pick it up, glance at a few pages, and suddenly I can feel the old blood and vigor churning; I get nervous, restless, excited, and in a few moments I am loudly damning the whole world and raising my voice to heaven—it takes me sometimes an hour or two to calm down after just seeing the thing lying on a table.

I suppose I have to take a good bit of blame for it, though. Truly, I asked for it when I came back home and left it. That was mistake number two. Number one was ever writing it in the first place. . . .

Yours, Mac

To Max Steele, from Ormond Beach, Florida, July 2, 1959.

Dear Max,

. . . Congratulations on the goddamned stories and everything. Going off and holing up like that sounded to me an impossible way to write, and I still believe it is. But anyhow I'm especially interested in the children's book.* What is it like? If and when you get an extra copy of it, could you send me one? I would like to see how you went about it and try it out on the children. They love to read anyhow. Trena reads with *expression*.

As for myself, we are now, as you can see, in Florida, and have a fine place here. It's right on the ocean; there is plenty of room; I have a nice pool in the back, a garage apartment; you can fish in front in the surf and at night go to the dog races or jai alai or many other things, and I am going slightly nuts here. We've been here a month and I'm ready to leave. I'm so sick of vacationing I don't think I'll ever want another one. I'm doing no work—never even sit at the typewriter (this is probably the first personal letter I have written in three months)—and am becoming pretty depressed with the whole thing. Whether I like it or not, I think I'm going to have to make up my mind that I would be more satisfied writing than anything else and go ahead and do something about it. I want to go ahead and meet some other writers and get into the business. Can you realize that I only really know *two* writers? You and Styron. I've met some others of course—but this was only a matter of shaking hands and looking at them hard, or maybe having a drink, social chit-chat, and that shouldn't count. I knew Sigrid de Lima too, but have seen her only once in the past eleven years. Anyhow, I want to get into the business and meet some of them. It's hard to compete with anybody without looking them straight in the eye sometimes and that's something I would like to do.

Going to have to do something, though. Not long ago I got so down that I decided I had better go see a psychiatrist, and I did, and it didn't work out. For one thing, I think he thought I was crazy. Didn't seem to believe a word I said. I told him I had written a book and he doubted that. He also doubted I

* "Sam, the Hungry Goose" (unpublished).

had spent six years in the army, or that I had a college degree. He kept figuring around with dates and things, going to trap me that way. Anyhow, I think I finally convinced him that at least the facts were true, and then he said he knew what my whole trouble was immediately. He said it was a matter of my drinking three and four cans of beer at night. This was a crock and I let him know what I thought of it. He was convinced, though, and said that in eight weeks he could make a new man out of me and stop me from drinking beer. He said he probably could do it in four, but that he could give a cut-rate for the eight-week treatment ($150) whereas the four weeks cost $100. This was to be in advance, he said, so that we wouldn't have to worry about money. Myself, I wasn't worried about money. Anyhow, I finally decided on the four-weeks treatment, but after I got back to the house, I decided against the whole thing. He sounded too much like Charles Atlas to me and if all he can do is stop me from drinking beer, I don't care to fool around with him anyhow. I like to drink beer and I'm not going to let a fool like him talk me out of it. He might be sane as hell, but he's not too bright, and that ought to count for something too.

But I am hard-up right now. About the only writing I have done this year is a little sketch for the teen-age girl next door in Cordele for her to do in a beauty contest—Miss Watermelon Queen, I think it was.* She didn't have any talent for the talent portion so I wrote her a thing ridiculing those who do have talent. Then I wrote one long letter to a teen-aged newspaper editor who wondered if I would write a little article about teen-aged problems, growing up and so on. He was a real smoothie, the way his letter read, and I ripped his little head off his shoulders with a letter that might be entitled *To Hell With Teen-Agers and Their Problems.* I was sick of hearing them discussed. What else could be said about growing up that hadn't been said a million times? *Don't* grow

* The girl's name was Jan Hamilton.

up? But I never mailed it as I lost his address, and I was glad later I did. I might have given him a teen-age trauma, and I wouldn't want to be responsible for anything like that.

Anyhow, that has been the extent of my literary out-put this year, chewing out one teen-ager and helping another one to get to be a Miss Watermelon. But I can't blame that on three cans of beer at night.

I'm certainly glad to hear, though, that you have finally decided to settle down somewhere and open a health food store along with Mexican crafts. This sounds to me the most sensible idea you have had in years. It's too bad you didn't recognize your true bent years ago. You might not have wasted so much time writing books and stories—probably today you could have been a health food and Mexican craft tycoon if you had begun a little earlier. Anyhow, I was glad to hear it. Up until I read that, I thought *I* was hard-up.

Let me hear from you when you get the chance. Wouldn't want you to delay any of your Mexican crafts, but if you feel like writing again, I would like to hear. I am seriously thinking about moving the whole family somewhere around New York this fall, but will be here for awhile anyhow. Thanks again for writing.

Mac

P.S. You don't know a good psychiatrist who drinks, do you?

To Max Steele, from Weston, Connecticut, late October, 1959.

Dear Max,

Your whereabouts are a little confusing too. Am glad anyhow to hear that you are back in New Orleans as you seemed to like that place. Also it is much easier spelled than some of those Mexican places.*

As for my whereabouts, I think I know less about that than I do about yours.† We are now located in this little town north of Westport, which is, I understand, in the state of Connecticut. This is just north and east of New York where I thought we were going to be located about this time. You actually can never tell where you are going to end up on these freeways, though, especially with the children becoming delinquents right in the car, one car following the other, and everybody hungry, tired, and disagreeable. Anyhow, we have a house here about four miles north of the motel where we spent a miserable week holed up in motel rooms, an experience I never care to go through again with children. It got to the point nobody even wanted to go out and eat. I had to haul meals back and forth. Finally got the house, though, the only restriction by this time being absolute Immediate Occupancy. Most of these liesurely sons-of-bitches up here want two and three weeks to move with us crammed up in those motel rooms.

But we got the place and I am stuck with nearly a years lease and don't even like the place. The house is all right, but it is rural—or at least what they call rural, though God knows how anybody up here ever made a living farming as I see nothing but fields of rocks—and more isolated than Cordele. Also, I feel like walking on tip-toes most of the time. Everything is very picturesque and quaint. I hope to God I never see anything quaint again as long as I live. Even old cows up here are supposed to be quaint.

Anyhow, I am not doing nothing much. I wanted very much

* Steele had spent the summer in Mexico, chiefly in Cuernavaca.
† By August of that year, Hyman had firmly decided to settle the family somewhere near New York and to look for some sort of job which did not involve writing. Finding no job, he remarks wryly in this letter, "Somebody's lost a damn good clerk."

to get a job, but I can't find one. I run into the same thing everywhere. "If you write a script (or story or article, etc.) we'll be glad to look at it." Which is just what I don't want to do right now. All I want is a simple job, but when I bring it up, everybody thinks I'm crazy. If I don't get something soon, I'm going back home, lease or not. Somebody's lost a damn good clerk, but if they didn't want to take advantage of my offer, it's their hard luck.

Most of the people around are in advertizing, insurance, things like that; and all of them are analyzing themselves. Even the preacher (who incidentally is from a little town in Georgia near Cordele) came by and explained apologetically, it seemed to me, how he became a preacher, but also announced proudly that he had studied psychology and was analyzing himself too. All of them are well-read, though, so we have book discussions. This is usually a matter of picking around until you discover you have read a book that the other person hasn't read, and then discussing that one for hours. All you can do is sit there and twitch. But when you get to the point that the simple enumeration of likes and dislikes of this book or that book passes for literary discussion, it's pretty irritating to discuss books anyhow to me.

We haven't seen anybody much outside of neighbors except the Styrons—they live about an hour's drive from here. And we've only seen them twice. Peter Matthiessen was up there with his girl when we went up, and after awhile we naturally began talking about Negroids, and before it was over, I found myself coming out strongly in favor of lynching. This didn't make a very good impression, I don't think, but it did give me the idea (or help me with it as I had it before) of writing a TV script to that effect. But nothing came of it. I talked to some people at CBS about it; I told them I had sometimes seen as many as four programs on the straight on TV coming out solidly against lynching, and I thought I might just do one coming out *for* it. The peculiar thing, though, was that even though they seemed a little horrified, in a day or two I got a call from California from a man out there who was actually interested. Nothing has been done, though.

Now I have an apology to make. About your story.* I could explain this a lot better if I could see you, but I know you can visualize it if you take into consideration that the children had your story in Florida and it got packed with their stuff, that we went from there to Georgia where I finally located it in a closet with their toys while we were getting ready to pack and come up here, that we were about two weeks getting this place, and that I have been searching for it ever since. I think now that it is back in Cordele. So I didn't get to send it where you said to send it even though I really did try. When and if we get back to Cordele, I'll try again.

Damned glad to hear about the story in Esquire.† I'll be looking for it. I was down there the other day too, looking for a job.

No other news that I can think of. Styron has finally finished his book; ‡ it is now at the publishers. They were down the other night and he talked a little worried about it, but I didn't put much stock in it. He seemed relieved but restless. Spent most of the night playing set-back.

As for exchanging ten pages a week, I'll be glad to give it a try. It's no fair cheating, though. You can't send out ten pages you wrote five years ago. Also, I think it might be a good idea to take the same theme. (I mean *broad* theme.) Then you could write it the way you saw it, and then I could write it the way it *really* was. But I'm not particular. Anyway you want to do it is fine. We might could do it even as a matter of collaboration. Why don't you send ten pages and we'll see what happens. . . .

As ever, Mac

* "Sam, the Hungry Goose."
† "The Silent Scream," *Esquire*, LIV (September, 1960), 172–75.
‡ *Set This House on Fire.*

To Max Steele, from Weston, Connecticut, November 16, 1959.

Dear Max,

I'm behind in my homework already. I narrowed it down from ten pages to five pages and now to ten lines, but I couldn't write anything to any extent right now if I described every leaf in the yard seperately and in detail. Everything is all fouled up. I am leaving tomorrow for California, taking the jet out—Gwendolyn's mother is comin up here to help her pack, and then they'll drive back to Cordele. I'll be back there by the middle of December, crazy as a loon probably. This TV thing cropped up again, and now I've got to go tearing ass across the country at six hundred miles per hour to do something I don't care anything about doing in the first place. But that's the story of my life. . . .

Was up at Styron's the other night and chit-chatted (argued is the word) with Robert Penn Warren, and met a friend of yours, Thomas Ginsburg [Guinzburg].* We raked you over the coals good and proper. (I'm just kidding. Nobody would say anything nasty because everybody was afraid somebody else might be a friend of yours. Which I hated because I had several things to say.) Anyhow, I have [had] enough of it up here. The men are like women and the women are like men. The women don't even wear dresses anymore, only slacks and blue jeans (ugly ones too, like they've been out in fields.) and have mighty strong opinions on every subject. I've found myself twice now in the ridiculous position of arguing against women's suffrage. Can't help it, though. They just bring it out in me. But Goddamn ugly women with opinions.

I've been offered a job by the *Atlanta* (that shouldn't be

---

* Formerly managing editor of the *Paris Review;* now owner of Viking Press, Inc. in New York.

underlined) Constitution (that should) that I might take. (Excuse this paper. I figure my paper very closely, and just used the last page before leaving.) I can go where I want and do what I want to do, and write columns about it. I'm going to talk with them about it when I get back from California. It sounds good. If I'm lucky, I can get to be a sports writer. But the main thing is I can just go any place that interests me and write about it and get paid for it. I don't know whether I can do it or not, but it does sound worth trying. . . .*

Anyhow, will let you know. By the way, where in the hell are your ten pages.

Yours, Mac

To James Oliver Brown, from Cordele, May 18, 1960.

Dear Jim,

. . . Have been reading more lately, but have gotten a stomach full of the modern kind of novel that you finish gladly, a little ashamed you are a human being. I have now turned back to anything that has a tinge of adventure and wholesomeness where people have feelings instead of opinions. There is something sick about all that. I don't want to read anything else about liberals, Jews, or homosexuals—either for or against. And I don't care to read anything else that is called complex but is really confused. There's a hell of a difference. But I suppose if I don't care to read it, I should write something different myself. . . .

Yours, Mac

* Hyman rejected the offer, believing the financial return insufficient.

To Max Steele, from Cordele, May 24, 1960.

Dear Max,

. . . I wish you could be going on this trip.* It sounds ridiculous for me to be going, but I think it is better than spending a summer loafing around Florida. I went down to Florida and spent awhile looking at whiskey stores and laundromats, thinking I might be happier with some kind of business, but never did find what I wanted. Maybe this will get me back to writing. I know I got interested again for the first time in a long time when I went up to Blackburn's literary meet; maybe it will do some good. I frankly don't have too much interest in Greece, but I think the trip might be fun anyhow.

By the way, you should have gone to that literary meet. I've never heard such crap. I sat on the panel with three teacher-writers and it really was a contest to see who could find the most symbols. It didn't make any difference whether the story was any good or not, the one that had the most symbols carried the day. And actually none of the stories were any good. I personally would have welcomed a straight mystery, comedy, adventure story or anything; there would have been something refreshing about it. But all of them seemed scared to death of action of any sort (or even movement); all the characters were deep thinkers; and you never really cared whether Uncle Clarence died at the end or not. (Only in these stories nobody ever dies either. That is too much action. You just *hint* they died.) I don't think I ever want to read another self-conscious literary story again. And the miserable thing about it was (at least to me) that here these teachers sat scanning stories and finding symbols by the dozen and there

* When the Hymans were at the arts festival at Duke in April of this year, I was delighted to learn that Mac might like to join me on my projected trip to Greece in June. Afterwards I wrote, urging him to make reservations. He made them, albeit I had no assurance in the meantime that he was actually coming on the voyage until I saw him aboard the ship.

the students sat, big eyed with wonder at how many symbols they could get in a story and not even know it, without even *trying*, by God! I guess I was the only sour note in it and Blackburn didn't like it too much, I'm afraid. But when you read a story about a young boy experiencing his first lynching, and you don't find out until right near the last paragraph, when the little boy starts to put his hair in pin-curls, that this is not about a little boy at all, but about a little girl, this to me should be pointed out. I don't care if the story has twenty-eight more symbols than the one before it, I would like to know immediately if it is a little boy or a little girl talking, and not be jolted in the nearly last paragraph. Anyhow, that's the way the whole thing went. In one story there was the sentence, speaking of a Christmas party, saying, "Aunt Clara, being dead, would not be here this year." It is hard for me to pass a sentence like that and keep a somber outlook that the story insisted on. All the rest of the story I was trying to re-write that sentence, if possible. How could you do it? "Aunt Clara, being dead, probably would not be here this year." "Aunt Clara, being dead, absolutely would not be here this year." It has all sorts of possibilities.

By the way, I read your story, The Glass House, in Harper's, and liked it very much.* Why don't you drop humor for awhile and go ahead and write serious stuff? That certainly came over well. You handle crazy people and horrible things suspiciously well.

Speaking of crazy people, did I tell you I tried a psychiatrist? Nothing so far has come of it, and I think he has given up and I have too. At first, we argued about integration and things like that; then we argued about psychiatry; finally I had to cancel one week and he had to cancel the next two weeks —then he cancelled this week's and I'm going to cancel next week. So all in all, I only went up about seven times over a

* "The Glass-brick Apartment," *Harper's Magazine*, CCXX (April, 1960), 60–65.

three months period, and we never got anywhere. He finally said he would like to talk to G. and he told her that he didn't understand me at all and didn't think he ever would, which gave me a peculiar glow of pleasure, for some reason or other, because I felt by this time that I understood him very well. And he's a damned nice fellow. But he either, I think, decided it was hopeless or that I didn't need it. I couldn't tell which. Possibly, though, my attitude wasn't what it should have been. It seemed to me that if you were going to get any help, you were going to have to start off by admitting you were hopelessly nutty, and I was willing to do that, but at the same time had to insist that if I was, he probably was too. . . .

I have been enjoying myself lately, mainly I think because of the ulcer. It gave me an excuse to quit trying to do things I didn't want to do, so I have been going in for all sorts of games, which I enjoy anyhow. Started back playing poker and did well at that for awhile (I was averaging about fifty dollars a week with that for a couple of months.)—then I began losing and quit and started playing golf and tennis again. Then the fish started bedding and we did a good bit of fishing, and G. taught me how to play bridge. You ever play bridge? Myself, I have thoroughly enjoyed it. We've been playing about three nights a week, and even though I don't know the rules well, I do know enough about it now to get a kick out of it. It's a hell of a good game. . . .

Yours, Mac

To his wife, from aboard the S.S. ——, bound for Piraeus, June 11, 1960.

Dearest Gwendolyn,

Notice the date & now guess where I am. We're just pulling out of New York harbor. It's been the damndest mess I've ever seen. Will tell you about it as I go along.

Had a fairly nice trip up on the train, but didnt get much

sleep. Sat in the bar & talked to a naval officer—a skin-diver until late, then, his being from Chicago, about integration naturally. So didn't sleep much.

Saw Jim [Brown] for about an hour. Also called Bob Loomis who as usual was tied up but wished I had let him know I was coming. Then got a taxi, picked up my bags from the station & came on out to the ship. Lots of confusion, but not of the good kind, so I was tired. Blackburn showed up later (we're in the same room); then I had to go hunt my bags which were sent to the wrong room. The cabin itself is all right; we share it with a fellow from Israel about my age & a Rabbi from New Jersey who wears a beard and is an overbearing old bastard expecting to be waited on. Blackburn, Hooper * (younger than I am & very shy) and I are the only gentiles I have seen. I think there are supposed to be 3 others, but haven't seen them.

Anyhow, we got out Saturday [Thursday] about seven after more confusion—this time with a tug-boat; they got fouled up somehow & had to chop the rope with an axe & it exploded like a shotgun. B. went to bed about nine; I went up & drank beer in the bar. (Previously they had a get-together party which I left as soon as possible) then I watched several young girls trying to play bridge, & when one of them dropped out, I played about three hands myself. They were so bad that to them I was an expert. They were also quite embarrassed to learn I wasn't Jewish, it seemed.

Anyhow, I got a fairly good nights sleep & the next morning, it was getting rough. Many sick. Tried to teach Bl. how to play gin rummy, but he doesn't know much more about cards than Tom [Hyman] & was a little sick besides. After lunch (the food is lousy; the service worse.) it began to get much rougher, so I spent my time trying to read or sleep. Was going to write you a letter, but too rough. Then about 5 or 6, I went

---

* Robert Hooper, who had been teaching modern languages at Duke, was on his way first to the Middle East, then to the American School of Classical Studies in Athens to study for a year.

up to the deck where everybody was wrapped up in the chairs. By this time, it was so rough that they had strung up ropes to hold when you walk. Anyhow just as I was reaching the top of the stairs, there was [a] jolt that sounded like dynamite & it seemed as if the ship was going to slam out of the water. Right above me, I saw a man literally sailing across the floor from one side to the other. Then there were glasses breaking, chairs falling, screaming—real pandemonium. I ducked my head under the stairs in case of glass, then ran up to the outer deck that the man had sailed through (they had the deck chairs on the starboard side—not in the rear) & found him lying on the floor, completely unconscious, bleeding from the head & ear. And by this time, there seemed to be panic everywhere. One woman was screaming for her baby which scared hell out of me as I thought it had gone overboard. Then another little girl was screaming for her mother while they tried to help her through the doors back inside. I finally got her by one arm & helped get her in; then tried to help another man put the rope back, but it was torn off. For a little bit, I thought it was going to be a *Titantic* as the ship was still pitching & rolling all over the place. People hollering, children crying. Went down to the cabin to see if everything was all right—trunks and chairs thrown all around but calmer. Then back up to see about the man again (they had some men trying to carry him when I left) & watched him, still unconscious, being hauled in.

Meanwhile the weather got worse & you couldn't find out a damned thing that was going on, tried to eat but impossible; the plates would slide across & hit the floor. Finally gave it up & went back to the cabin.

At this time, the wind seemed to change as the boat was now leaning in the opposite way & the waves (many of them going slam over the third deck) were beating against our side like tons of cement. Water poured in until we got it fixed. I decided by then that we had gone through a low (in which the wind would change direction) & were now on the other side.

Anyhow it was a hell of a night. I went up & got a beer & took a tranquilizer to try to sleep, but it was mainly a matter of holding on all night. But this morning it was calm, & I felt some better. It wasn't until after breakfast, though, that I found out my theory about the low was completely wrong; that we had turned around during the night & were headed back to Boston or N.Y. (they didn't announce a thing that I heard). They cleared the deck for a helicopter (to pick up the unconscious man who seems to be in serious shape). Then a recon plane flew over & decided it couldn't be done. So we finally came all the way back to N.Y. harbor where a small boat came out & picked him up, still unconscious.* We just turned around & are going back out again now, even though I felt inclined to get off with him. I thought I would try to call, also, but they never berthed.

So everything so far has been miserable. We eat with two older couples that I could have gotten along without knowing. (One of the women said today, spitting out watermelon seeds, "I don't like to eat much because it makes me belch.") I'm glad I'm getting off in Greece.

(Mon.) Didnt get to finish this, so will just start another. I plan to mail this & the next at Gibraltar, so will just continue on next letter.

You don't know how much I miss you & the children. I dont feel that I'll stay as long as I thought. Actually, I find all this pretty tiresome so far. Nothing to do on this ship much except listen about Israel.

Incidentally, no hot & cold stewardesses, only two scrub-women & a bunch of Marjorie Morningstars.

I love you, Mac

* The man, a young Greek, later died in the hospital. His bereaved parents met the ship at Piraeus, and Hyman was the first to offer condolences. As an eyewitness, he tried to describe to them what had happened.

To his wife, from S. S. Aegaeon, July 1, 1960.

Dear Honey,

Wrote to you last after Crete. Then sent the pictures (did you get them) from Rhodes, the next day, the place that I liked most of all. Went on a tour of Rhodes in the morning & took the aft. off to bum around by myself while the tour continued on to other ruins which I have seen enough of for awhile. I went swimming (but only for a few minutes as the wind was blowing & was too cold) then spent the rest of the day wandering around the streets. Very interesting place too. The old city—a large size place where a few thousand people live—is just as it was when it was finished during the Crusades. The whole place is completely walled in like a fort; the streets—no larger than sidewalks in places—were made by pebbles stuck in the ground—and, as I say, people are still living there with everything pretty much as it was, in the ruins. I walked for hours all through the place, got lost several times, but really enjoyed it. We stayed until after midnight, so went in town after supper to see the night-life, ended up going to a movie ("A Hole in the Head" with Frank Sinatra). The movie was constructed simply by putting a wall next to another building, a screen in front & projector at the rear. No top at all. Between the changing of films they go up & down the aisles selling drinks, ice-cream, etc.

Yesterday was a rat-race. Up about seven to see the town of Hallicarasis [Halicarnassus], Turkey, which was a very desolate place. Ruins & a mosque. Two hours there, then sailed for Cos island which was better. But after two hours there we were off for the next island, Patmos, where we stayed until about twelve last night. The idea was to go up on donkeys to see a monastary & some nuns (St. John was supposed to have written the Apocolypse there, but I doubt it;), but I didn't go. Very steep, it looked, & the heights make me uncomfortable anyhow. B. went & walked back, right upset over the steepness

& the donkeys. Besides I cared nothing about seeing more ruins & nuns anyhow. I sat around the town for a while, walked some, came on back to the ship. Pretty tired too. Too much for one day.

This morning the tour is at an uninhabited island where there *used* to be some ruins. I can see it now out the window. Small place with nothing but rocks, not a tree on the island. Even B. passed this one up. Myself, I couldn't see much point in going to an uninhabited island except to inhabit it for a few hours. . . .

I love you, Mac

To his wife, from aboard S. S. Massalia, bound for Naples, July 2, 1960.

Dear Hon,

It is now mid-night & I am in the bar of the Massalia, Greek Ship, drinking a beer. They had the movie *The Brothers Karamazov* which I just left, & which I was just [as] excited over this time as the other times I saw it. God, I wish I could write like that.

Today has been pretty hectic. Got into Athens this morning about eight, had to get laundry, mail, tickets, then back to Piraeus by eleven to catch this boat. Made it all right, but it was pretty much of a rush. B. rather upset over my leaving. I don't know how I'm going to like traveling alone either. Probably gets fairly lonesome. But I've enjoyed today, being by myself for a change. There are 3 others in the cabin with me (Greek, I think) but they were out most of the day so this aft. I spent reading a murder novel & napping. Eat at a table with an Englishman—just the two of us. Meals all right so far.

This is a peculiar ship. Very small (to show the movie, they tacked up a screen on deck) & only two classes. The tourist

class not only sleep on deck on the floor, they even have to fix
their own food, which seems to be mainly bread & coffee out
there too—and there are probably 200 of them jammed together. Some of them have only a sack for a pillow. I'm the
only American on board—the rest seem to be Greek, French,
Spanish, Italian, etc. Right now I'm the only one up, it seems.
And only one light here in the bar. . . .

I love you, Mac

To his wife, from Rome, July 16, 1960.

Dear Hon,

 . . . Anyhow, I have been enjoying it. Am now out at Jo's
place where I have been since Thurs.* I was coming out
Wednesday, but that morning two of the girls that were on
the ship—college girls—dropped by to see me, & I went with
them out to the Sistine Chapel & Vatican which they had
missed. I really appreciated their coming by & enjoyed being
with them (Jo & Angelo were coming back from the moun-
tains & pick me up either Wed. or Thurs.) Anyhow, Jo called
later that aft. & offered to drive me to Styron's on Thursday, &
I took her up on it. (I wrote you, I think, that Styron was at
the beach) Anyhow I came out with Jo & we drove down
there—a trip that turned out to be over 80 miles one way on
these little narrow roads—about 3 hrs.—which I would never
had considered taking if I had known it was going to be so
long. Besides being hot as hell. But we finally found the place,
& while Jo went to visit a friend of hers, I went with Styron &
Rose for more sightseeing after lunch. . . .

 Anyhow, after that we left—Jo driving all the way—& came

* Signora Angelo Bettoya is the former Josephine Patterson of Millen,
Georgia, a contemporary of Mitzi Hyman's at Wesleyan College, Macon.
Signor Bettoya owns several hotels in Rome.

back here (another 3 hrs.) both of us whipped. And then they had company for dinner—an editor, who could speak a little English & his wife—then some others who dropped in for drinks. Got to bed late—too tired to sleep, lay there & throbbed until nearly daybreak.

I can't tell you, though, how nice they have been to me. They really have a beautiful place—about 8 miles outside Rome on [a] hill from which you can see the city; and when I got back, the maid (3 maids & one butler-waiter-helper, all trained like boat stewards) had not only hung up my clothes but had washed the dirty things. Have my own room & bath—this is a large house; the help stays in—& they couldn't have been nicer. I found I had left the coat to my suit at Styron's & Angelo sent a telegram to have it brought back by one of their friends who is coming here on Sunday. (So I'll have to stay until Monday anyhow now even though I was planning on leaving Sunday.)

Anyhow the next day I used Jo's car & went into Rome to get mail & try to shop. Got lost several times & the shopping was hopeless—all I could find were dolls that cost $30 & bottles of whiskey; but I put in most of the day at it, managed to get back here late in the aft. Then some cousin of Angelo's came over with his fiancée & we went to a night club down the road & had drinks & talked until about two. The cousin could speak no English, his fiancée a little, but it was nice even though I was damned tired at the end of it. So lay awake & throbbed again.

But have had it easier today. Slept late & Jo went in with me this time to shop & I at least got some of it done. Got you a little something I hope you'll like. At least I do. And I picked it out too. Had lunch with Angelo at his hotel (and was presented with a fishing rod he had gone out & bought for me because I had expressed some interest in his, never saw such hospitality.) Anyhow, have napped for about two hours this afternoon & feel better. They are still napping, I think.

Going out for supper tonight to Travastere [Trastevere] where they have the poetry contests & everything that we saw.* . . . God knows I miss you & the children—even Florida. And I want to settle down & work so bad, I'm miserable about it. In that sense, maybe this trip will be worth it after all. Will stop now.

I love you, Mac

To Josephine and Angelo Bettoya, from Venice, July 23, 1960.

Dear Angelo & Jo,

Will write later, but wanted to write now while it is still fresh with me to thank you for all you did for me. I don't know when I have been treated so downright royally; it makes me feel a little ashamed that the best we can do—when & if you ever get to Georgia—is to take you out to Daphne Lodge for cat-fish. But I do hope sometimes to have a chance to do that.

Been reading the books you let me have & like most of what I see—particularly that Tucci. He really *can* write, can't he. I read the one about *This Very Rich Woman* & was pretty impressed with it. Wish I could read some of the Italian. So far, though, about the best I can do is order a glass of cold milk.

The fishing rod incidentally has come [in] very handy. I make it a point of carrying that myself & most people—not knowing whether you are going to punch at or hit at them with it—give you a wide berth & show a lot more respect. Coming in on the gondola, I was much tempted to take it out & go through the motions of casting down the Grande Canal, but didn't have the necessary drink I would need before doing something like that.

* On their visit to Rome, summer, 1956.

I like Venice, but am now ready to leave. I can take pigeons just so long, particularly when they are as arrogant as they are here. I have been wanting to pot one of them, have it cooked & served right in one of those restaurants in St. Marks. Then somebody could take a snapshot of somebody eating a pigeon in St. Marks Square instead of feeding one. I actually was planning on getting out of here yesterday, but didn't get the right reservations—leaving later this afternoon for Paris.

Better close as I have to get this to the Post Office & pack, etc. Just wanted to say thanks again for everything. Will let you know later how fishing is on the Seine—I have great plans.

As ever, Mac

To his wife, from Venice, July 23, 1960.

Dear Honey,

. . . Venice is still pretty, but gets old quick. I have been over to Lido to the gambling casino (but didn't gamble), to the Bienalle [Biennale]—modern arts festival—which I thought was pure bunk & wandered around. Yesterday I bumped into the Israeli group & had lunch with about eight of them & the guide who is a nice fellow. A long & tiring meal but it was good to have the company. Was going back out to the modern art thing with them—they all talk about it as if they know something about it & I was really interested to see what they could find to say about a canvas with a croker-sack hanging on it—but then one of them—my favorite out of the group—showed up with a toothache, the whole side of her face swollen, worried to death. So instead of the arts thing, I helped her find a dentist, & it turned into a real farce. The dentist couldn't speak English & this girl was frantic over the idea that they were going to pull it. I finally had to go down to

Cook's, right down stairs, to get somebody to translate. And it worked out all right. It turned out he just wanted to fill it, which he did all right.

Anyhow, for some reason or other, the whole thing exhausted me. Having helped find the dentist, I got to feeling somewhat responsible naturally & began to be afraid they might start pulling teeth. Was damn relieved when it was over & so worn out, I went back to the hotel & just conked out. I just can't take responsibility it seems. . . .

Might call from Paris. Won't try it again from here. Tell the children I can't wait to get back & go swimming with them. I miss you all more than I can say. Let me hear.

I love you, Mac

To Josephine and Angelo Bettoya, from Ormond Beach, Florida, August 11, 1960.

Dear Jo and Angelo:
 I am finally back, but have been moving at such a clip for such a length of time (or so it seems to me) that I'm having a hard time now not making plans to start moving again. Flew back from Paris which I did not like much more than the first time I was there. I think you're right when you say those people are mean. I thought they were mean and I couldn't even understand what they were saying. . . .

As ever, Mac

To his wife, from New York, September 25, 1960.

Dear Hon
 . . . Today, I slept late, ate breakfast, and took a long walk up to Columbia—about forty blocks in all, then came back here to read the paper and maybe write some more, but

instead dozed off for about an hour. I think it's because I took one of those tranquilizing pills before breakfast, which I haven't been doing at all. Been taking one only at night. Hope it doesn't mess my hours up again.

One thing I got to thinking about, though, today while I was walking (which, in my present condition, might not be thinking at all, but only excuses) was that maybe I had been making the same mistake here as I made at home. And that if there is any truth in that, I could write there as well as here. That is, that instead of writing what I know and see at the moment, I keep going back and trying to construct novels and stories out of the past. This naturally throws me into a quandary because things out of the past are not immediate with me, not the thing that I am highly concerned with at the moment. Yet I always avoid writing about what is around me *now* with the idea, I guess, that I don't have perspective on it. I don't mean by that the actual physical environment—that I should write about that necessarily—but whatever feeling the environment and people around bring out. For example, I guess my best writing over the past few years has been in letters when I am telling somebody what I have been doing, what I have been seeing. Max Steele is always mentioning my letters—which one is funnier than the other—and I remember one time Mr. Linscott said that I never had to worry about publishing anything because if worse came to worse I could always publish my letters. The thing about this that interests me is that when I write letters I am always writing about the *present*, what is going on and what I feel *now*. Then I got to thinking about NTFS and remembered then too, that even though I was writing this about a boy I knew years before,* a lot of that was simply writing to you what I

---

* The original Will Stockdale, whom Hyman met either on a train or at an induction center. Details vary, but all of Hyman's accounts agree on the boy's innocence, his ignorance, and his fierce love of independence—"If they'll leave me alone, I'll leave them alone." The army left him alone. See John Pennington, Atlanta *Journal*, October 9, 1954, p. 10; Marti Martain, Greenville (N.C.) *Reflector*, November 17, 1962.

was seeing at that moment out at the base in Houston. Or if not actually seeing, at least experiencing, because as you remember my whole feeling back then was that the Korean War and everything about it was a farce, and this was brought home to me every day. Then I also remembered that much of Hemingways stuff was written right after or during whatever happened that he wrote about. (I don't mean like a diary of course. I mean it was fresh to him.) For example, The Sun Also Rises was almost immediately on the scene he had just left; the Fifth Column was, and many of the others. He was even discussing the people he was going to write about, what they said and how they were, with Gertrude Stein while they were still there. This is also true of Tolstoy in Anna Karenina when he went right home from seeing a woman killed and began writing a story about her, in the first spark of inspiration. Faulkner has done this a good bit too, no doubt, living in and writing about the same place.

Well, this is one thing I *haven't* been doing. I keep trying to go back and construct novels out of the past that I don't really feel anything about anymore; and I shouldn't write that way. Being a person who is pretty well smothered by his environment when I'm in it, I should write about what comes naturally to me then and there. Not just about the things of course—mainly about the feelings. The 100th Cent. for example came from a remark I heard in that class I was going to, right then.* The story itself did too almost; I just moved it to another place and showed it the way I saw it. And of course those little things for Jan † were done in the same way, something that was going on *now*, in the present.

This doesn't mean I shouldn't write about the past at all. That will all come up—I know I remember things that tie into any argument or situation after I get started with something—and I can always use that. But that is natural remem-

* See letter of November 12, 1950, above.
† See letter of July 2, 1959, above.

bering without trying to remember—it just comes up. You know it does, for example, when we have an argument. We might be fussing over whether or not you have bought me any sardines—and that is the *immediate, present* thing that gets me started, but then I can go back a hundred years and support my outlook or argument with things I thought I had forgotten. Well, why shouldn't writing work the same way? It's the *immediate* thing that gets me started—that gives me my viewpoint and outlook (which I need far, far more than any material)—all the other stuff will come after I have started. Didn't Cervantes do this same thing with Don Quixote; he was disgusted with the present romances, and that gave him his start. All the rest came easy, it seems, once that start and viewpoint was established.

I suppose what I am doing, in a way, is hunting for an excuse to come home and try writing again. But do you think I am wrong in what I say above? *Read it carefully now and think about it*. Isn't there some truth in it? It is true that I am lonesome and want to come back, but I think this is true too, though, don't you? And if it is, couldn't we somehow work something out looking at things that way? I will still need to do things, see people, be a part of life even to get excited over anything anyhow—will *have* to do that—but if what I have said is true, don't you think that could be done. I could write almost like a journalist (which might be better as there will be no self-consciousness over ART) and let come from it what will. For example, I feel that right now what I could write best is something about a person being alone in New York. It would be a miserable, self-pitying novel, but I could do it, I think. And things I see all the time set me off the same way. I was on a bus the other day with a driver the like of which I never saw before; he made announcements like an airplane pilot, gave temperature, weather forecasts, told the passengers to hold to their seats now, this was going to be a little bumpy, when he went over some gravel or something—I could have done a story about him maybe. He was pretty funny. Also walking in Times Square I saw another hell of a sight—one of these old men beatniks with floating grey hair and beard arguing right up in the face of one of the most comical looking drunks I have ever looked at. It seems the drunk had said something about education and the old man was going to show him who was the smartest. So right up in his face he said, "All right, what's one and one?" "Two," the drunk said with this kind of pleased blissful happy look on his face. "What's two and two?" "Four." "Four and Four." "Eight." 8 and 8. "16" and so on right at the top of his voice when he said, "Sixty-four and sixty-four" and the drunk, blinking his eyes still smiling, hesitated and finally said, "I'll bet you don't even know that one yourself."

And this set the old man off. For ten minutes after that he doubled figures at the top of his voice, right up in the drunks face, while the drunk looked around with this expression on his face as if he wondered what on God's earth he had gotten himself into, apologetic almost, while the man kept shouting. This drew a crowd for awhile, and the old man was nearly hoarse from shouting, still doubling figures. And what broke it up was almost comical in itself. People were now standing in the street listening, and somebody said, with a car trying to get through, "Watch out or somebody is going to get hurt," and the old man heard this, misinterpreted it, and yelled at the top of his voice, "*Work?* I was working before you were born!" They finally had to get a policeman to break it up.

Now what I'm saying is that I see things all the time, day in and day out, that could make stories, but I never write them. At home, certainly I could have written about the Tax Equilisation meeting; I could have written about that preacher from Atlanta—many other things, but I have passed over them for some reason, have never done it. And maybe it is true I can't do it in Cordele either—certainly I have thought so long enough—but right now it is beginning to look to me that if I have other things to do outside the house, things to see, people, and would write about them, I might could do it there too. But I haven't thought it all out. I do think there is some truth in it, though, don't you? And maybe if I can't do it there, I can do it another place. But I do need activity and I need to write about what I feel and know *at the moment.* . . . And maybe, as I say, it is all an excuse to come home. Because despite the way I act sometimes, I do miss and love and need you and the children—and not just from lonesomeness either. I don't want to be smothered by it, or by writing either—I need to put both on a level where I am not dominated by either. I'll have to sometimes be able to put you and the children in the closet the way I used to do the writing when it became too serious. And of course I need to be able to put the writing there too every once in awhile. If I'm going to have any control over my life, I'm going to have to control, or dominate, those things which might can control me. I have to feel free to have either. . . . Will stop now.

Love you, Mac

To James Oliver Brown, from Cordele, November 21, 1960.

Dear Jim,

. . . Do you by any chance know of that Actor's Studio * where they have professional playwrights working on scripts? Herbert Gold [novelist and critic] told me about it and it sounded like a perfect thing for me when I was there, but was told they were filled up. I'd give anything to get into something like that where I could see other people writing and be writing myself. Couldn't think of anything better. . . .

Mac

* The Actors Studio in New York, N.Y.

To Alvin G. Manuel, from Cordele, December 9, 1960.

Dear Al:

. . . As for myself, I got wrapped up again in that first novel I wrote and worked on it again. Don't know whether you know Helen Hull or not; she used to teach at Columbia and was a pretty good critic, I thought. She read it and was all for my going ahead and publishing it; this excited me, and I went back to work on it with a little more enthusiasm. Finally bogged down on the last chapter, though, and now am in confusion about it again. I can't get it right somehow.

Also worked for a time on a comedy about a man going on a tour of Europe and liked what I was doing on that one. The first few chapters looked all right—even got tickled at some of it myself. . . .

Did you ever read the story I did called *The Hundredth Centennial?* That's one I still like. It runs about twelve thousand words, has a lot of characters, and I always had the idea that it could be made into a movie. With as much freedom as the movies are taking nowadays, it might be possible. Too sexy for TV, I know. . . .

Sincerely, Mac

To Max Steele, from Beverly Hills, California [December, 1960 ?].

Dear Max,

Thanks for the letter. As far as the TV goes, though, the way I am feeling now, I'd advise you not to break any kind of record by seeing a TV drama. My stomach is being turned pretty fast. This time I came out here with the understanding that they were going to do this thing pretty much the way I wanted. It turns out that they have no intentions of doing anything much more than one more of those goddamned B class things that turn your stomach when you think that you might be responsible for it. This thing I had was kind of wild farce and satire—one of them was a take-off on a crooked preacher, for example, who's in the preaching racket so he can write best sellers. He has written one that I call *The Power of Perverted Thinking,* and I had some fun with it, particularly when he gets so sick of this fellow he has baptized so much that he loses his temper and tries to drown him by holding him under too long in front of the whole congregation. Then, being as this causes something of a scandal, he tries to save his reputation by converting the meanest man in the county who turns out to be a very violent man who is awfully willing to be saved, but who can never tell whether he is saved or not until he lets somebody slap his cheek to see if he is capable of turning the other cheek. Usually he isn't—usually when they slap the one cheek, he loses his temper, beats hell out of and nearly kills the man that does it, and this is what the preacher finds himself up against. I'm not trying to give you a lot of stories, but only trying to point out what happens with something like this. Number 1: They are afraid of losing listeners who like Norman Vincent Peale. No. 2: Religion is too touchy anyhow. No. 3: It wouldn't be a very happy ending and would leave a bad taste in your mouth. And so on, just as an example.

Well, it turns out now that they want to have a sweet, innocent girl who just has a kind of nice, sentimental country outlook. Their first idea was that she would be married, see, and she would have this little house, see, and we would watch her doing all those crazy things that young wives do the first year of marriage, see; I mean you could have big cakes in ovens that just get bigger and bigger. All those crazy, crazy things, but with a pretty little touch at the end when this little wife straightens everything out and actually helps her husband get a raise, so you'll want to see it again next week.

Well, I said to hell with that and wrote one this last week in which a Mayor, kind of wholesomely crooked, is in financial trouble with the city—the books are in bad shape; the Inspector is coming in, etc. so in desperation he gets a cotton allotment on the municipal golf course and puts it in the soil bank to raise money. After a lot of hoop-de-do, it ends up with my heroine working things around so that the whole golf course is plowed up and planted in peach trees. Actually it is not as bad as it sounds. But can you guess the objections they have to it? 1. Too much emphasis on golf might antagonize people who like Eisenhower who plays golf. 2. Too drastic to plow up a golf course. 3. There is no love interest. 4. She, the heroine, should actually *save* the golf course and the Mayor in the end so that it will leave a good taste in your mouth. 5. There should be a young reporter in it that she will later marry and do all those crazy, crazy things young wives do, like cakes in ovens, etc.

So I am about ready to say to hell with it. What they want, without saying it, is corn of the worst sort—real sentimental corn at that—and I just don't have the insides for it. I wouldn't mind doing a good, rolicking hell-raising comedy—I could enjoy that. But I don't know how long I can take this crap. The way I feel now I'll probably be headed home in a week or so. I don't think we'll ever see eye to eye on it—if they'll just pay me now, I'm ready to call it quits. They owe me expenses and two thousand dollars for the script. And with all the expenses I've gone to, I need it. . . .

You'd like it out here, though, in a way. Friend of mine lives in a place that I think you ought to have—in the top of a merry-go-round. I was up there the other night and while people sat there and discussed art and politics, this merry-go-round kept going around and around with all that music playing. Began to seem a little wierd after awhile. Quite a few of them live up there, though. Several apartments. Everybody out here paints. There are slabs and gobs of paint everywhere, framed and hanging on walls. They all seem to appreciate it too, only every once in awhile one of them gets drunk and says confidentially it all looks like a lot of hog-wash, which it looks to me sober. Been reading a novel one of them wrote—a very serious novel with a very serious, bleeding-heart kind of hero, only for some reason or other, he named the hero "Quackenbush." He doesn't mean it as funny either. It jolts me everytime, though. I can't take anybody seriously named "Quackenbush." Could you? Good fellow, though. He's caused a lot of people out here to hate me by saying I'm a racist and telling them I don't care for integration, but after they get real indignant, he takes the wind out of their sails by telling them I'm a Jew. That seems to make things all right. Every once in awhile I see somebody standing around hating me, though, and I know what's happened.

Anyhow, I will let you know if anything turns up. Nothing will, though, I don't think, but me. And I might turn up in New Orleans anyday now. I'd like to sneak out of here tonight, in fact, only I haven't got my pay.

As ever, [unsigned]

To Max Steele, from New York, January 11, 1961.

Dear Max,

I have been meaning to write, but as usual I didn't get around to doing anything I had been meaning to do. Nevertheless, I have thought about writing quite a few times. But then I would think of you conked out sick with God knows what in the condition I last saw you, and it would come to me that you might be dead by now anyhow, so there didn't seem to be much point in writing, that being the case. . . .

I personally have been so fouled up here these last few months that I can hardly think most of the time. From New Orleans, I came on up here and holed up in a hotel room and for about two and a half weeks, I was writing and working like a mad-man. Then I got interested again in that old novel, knew suddenly how it should be worked, and even had big plans of getting it shaped up in a month or two and being done with it. Then, though, things were not going well at home—one of the kids not feeling well and G. worn out—so I packed up and went back and immediately bogged up in everything I was doing. After getting thoroughly bogged, I went down to Florida for a week to try to get started back, and nearly collapsed completely. So I came back to Cordele, nearly nuts by this time, and decided that I would go back to New York again and this time get me an apartment with the idea that I would come back after Christmas, get some writing done, and at the same time try to get a house to move the family up. So I came back for a few days and finally at least succeeded at the one job of getting an apartment lined up. Then back to Cordele again for December and Christmas, and just came back here a couple of days ago. Now I'm about ready to go home again. I would like to stick it out and try to get something done, though, if possible. Right now, though, I don't have a goddamned idea of anything I care about writing at all. I feel like a beginner without a thought in my head.

Did a lot of hunting over Christmas. G. got interested and I took her several times. Knocked down twenty-five doves my first day out, and never could do any better all the rest of the season, so I steadily went downhill. Was finally glad to see the season go out. . . .

As ever, Mac

To Max Steele, from Cordele, February 9, 1961.

Dear Max,

. . . Was hoping too we could get together in N.Y. But I was holed up in that apartment for about three weeks and thought I was going nuts with it. Couldn't get any work done at all. One of the worst trips I have ever had.

So I finally decided that I had enough of it, the whole thing, and that I was coming home and find me a job and give up writing—or at least, trying to. That seemed like a very good idea at the time. But after a few days of speculating around about various jobs with the idea of not even ever trying to write again, I found myself turning into something of a Zombie, kind of a walking dead man, and finally gave up and admitted I would try to write some more, even though I'm still speculating on the job. God knows I would like to have something to do. I know I get along better with some kind of work, and write better too. It seems that I write either easily or not at all, which is, I guess, the mark of an amateur; but it's a fact nevertheless, so I hope to find some other way to make a living and write only when I really want to. I've got enough of that damned desperate prose.

It really sounds good about your work. Hope Diana * doesn't let up on you at all and makes you sit down to it every day. . . .

What plans, if any, do you have? I realize that is a hard thing to figure all of a sudden, but thought you might have some. I am at such loose ends right now myself that I don't know really what I am going to do. I would like a job or a business, but I don't want to live here anymore. I want to sell this house and the one in Florida, get me a job somewhere so I will have something to do—preferably some place where there is somebody around who has read at least something besides Gone With The Wind, and try to settle for awhile. You wouldn't be interested in going in with me on a skating rink or a bar, would you? I don't much care where as long as the weather is not so bad. (That winter weather in N.Y. really got me this time. I felt like a prisoner in that apartment.) No

* Steele and Diana Whittinghill married in December, 1960, and were living in Ossining, New York.

kidding, if you want to go into something together, let me know. I'm damned tired of wandering around the world by myself. . . .

Mac

To Max Steele, from Cordele, March 10, 1961.

Dear Max,

. . . Let me say immediately, though, that—far from being annoyed with your letter—I appreciated it a hell of a lot. There are not that many people around who are interested enough in somebody else's doings to try to give them some advise. And most people around here that I know seem for some reason to feel that I am completely independent and that I don't need anybody's advise—or at least certainly hesitate to give it—so that I very seldom get an outside view of what I am doing or trying to do at all. And God knows, I need it just like anybody else. Anyhow, as I say, I appreciated it and have been wanting to ask you all about those rules of an alcholic that have meant so much to you. If they're that good, I intend to become an alcholic first chance I get—which should not be much trouble for me—so that I can then join AA. It certainly seems to be worth the doing.

As for that job, I have decided to go ahead and accept it.* It will mean moving over to Albany—I'll be working the rural areas around that section—and it'll be a pretty steady thing. Will have to get rid of this house and the one in Florida too, if possible, so I have quite a few things to think of right now. I am kind of looking forward to the work, though. I did something along this line the last time I was in the Air Force for a

* As counselor in the state vocational rehabilitation program. Hyman spent a week training for this job but then decided not to accept it.

few months, and it is the only kind of work that I ever did that I cared much about going into again. At that time I was working with parents and families of casualties; this time it will be working with handicapped of all sorts, trying to get them in shape to make a living on their own. Will have about a hundred clients, half white, half colored, so far as I can figure. Idea is to get them operated on, educated, trained, etc. and weaned away from welfare if possible. It seems pretty interesting to me. The people I have met in it seem to be pretty good people—most of the counselors have taken a cut in pay just to get into it. Believe it or not, Georgia actually leads the country in this sort of work, and they take a good bit of pride in it. I'm just hoping that I can do it and keep on with the writing too. If not, I don't know what I'll do. Probably quit the job and hop another boat for Europe, I guess. It's worth trying anyhow, though. . . .

Let me hear about your writing. Will be looking for the one in the *New Yorker;* * only they don't sell the *New Yorker* anywhere in this section of the country that I know of. They might possibly in Albany, though. . . . About the only interesting thing I have done in the past few weeks is playing a guitar. My kid sister, Dinah, has one and I began picking around with it, got a book of instructions and have learned to play it a little bit. So while I feel everything about me collapsing all over the place, I sit in the dark hours of the night (God knows I haven't been to bed before three and four in the morning in months now) picking out Red River Valley and Mack the Knife and such things on my guitar. I know just how Nero felt.

Let us hear from you.

As ever, Mac

* "The Cat and the Coffee Drinkers," *The New Yorker,* XXXIX (May 11, 1963), 105–19.

*To his sister Mitzi, from Sands Point, Long Island, Fall, 1961.**

Dear Sister,

. . . All the children doing fine in school. Gwyn's doing well in everything except arithmetic; Trena in nearly everything—although it's hard to tell,—and Tom still seems to enjoy himself. He was especially excited to find out they were going to have gym; he came in wild-eyed talking about it, and went out and practiced basketball all afternoon. G. didn't have the heart to tell him that they wouldn't have a basketball team in the first grade so he practiced hard for a couple of days. But he won the race and is the fastest one in his class anyhow, and the other day he came home and said that the teacher had called him up and asked him to read in the book and to keep reading until she stopped him. So he read the whole book to her, and now she has put him in the second book with the rest of the class still working on the first one. He is naturally still proud of himself, but coming up here has shaken him up a little bit in that people don't stop and talk to him all the time. He said the other day that in his class they had two Germans, two Italians, two from Norway or somewhere, and his teacher is Chinese—that he was the only American in the class. When I first brought him to New York, though—he and I rode on ahead, you might know—he kept speaking to people along the street and trying to carry on conversations with waiters until he saw that nobody was that interested. Then he said to me, "You know, Daddy, a lot of people up here don't know us, do they?" All he wants to do is go back to Cordele, I think. . . .

Love, Brother

---

* In the fall of 1961, Hyman again moved north, thinking that it might prove beneficial. However, he said it turned out to be "just about the worst life I have ever gotten into." His attempts at writing were unproductive; his wife was burdened with housework; and his landlord refused to agree to any compromise settlement on the two-year lease of the house.

To James Oliver Brown, from Cordele, May 3, 1962.

Dear Jim,

. . . As for myself, I am not doing anything much. Have lost interest almost completely in writing. I spent most of the hunting season hunting, and since that time I have become interested in golf again, and have been playing it from in the morning until late in the afternoon day after day.* No good at it, though. Actually, all I have succeeded in doing is wearing my hands nearly off—my fingers are so stiff in the mornings when I wake up that I can hardly move them and usually have to put them in water to relieve the swelling. Then I'll vow not to hit any more balls that day, but a little later will get to thinking about it, get bored and go out to the golf course again.

I've also looked into a couple of teaching jobs, but nothing looks promising along that line. I have also seriously considered going back into the army. I know better but I have been considering it anyhow. If I could get a decent rank, I think I would do it.

Of course, I miss the writing, but it is absolutely hopeless here. You ever try writing a letter to nobody about nothing? That's about the way my writing is nowadays, and reads like it too. It has gotten to the point where I despise the whole idea of sitting down at a typewriter.

I'm going to have to do something sooner or later, though, not only because I am bored silly with the ideal life of self-indulgence and recreation, but also because of financial reasons. I am still paying on the house in Florida, and still paying five hundred dollars per month for the house in New York.† This frankly is worrying the hell out of me. If I were living there it would be different, but the idea of sending five hundred a

---

* At this time, out of desperation over his insomnia and other problems, Hyman seems to have become obsessed with the idea of making his daily round of golf into an exhausting ordeal.
† The house at Sands Point, Long Island.

month to a man for an empty house is more than I can put up with. He keeps telling me he'll rent it out, but he never seems to get around to it. The bad thing is, my lease there still runs for nearly a year and a half. It makes me feel rather helpless. As a matter of fact, just thinking about it, I'm ready to go now back out to the golf course. . . .

As ever, Mac

To his daughter Gwyn,* from Cordele, June 29, 1962.

Dear Gwyn,

I wish you were back here to fuss at. Tom is the only one around now to get on my nerves and I am a little tired of fussing at him.

Was glad to hear about your winning the ribbons—all I ever won was a ping-pong tournament. Don't worry about winning things though—and for goodness sakes don't let those tests bug you; it really makes very little difference about the life-saving; if you don't pass it one time, you'll pass it another time. Just get a good rest; do what you want; it doesn't matter either whether you have all the fun on earth. It's hard going to a place where you don't know anybody. So just loaf & take it easy.

Tom has been sick but is all right now.

Do you like Lake Rabun? Your mama & I went over there & rode around in a boat after we left you & Trena. Pretty place.

No news except that the varmint Mushy has had kittens again and we can't—thank goodness—find them. Write.

Love, Daddy

* She was in a camp for girls at Clayton. Now married, she and her husband, John W. Ferguson, are students at Florida State University, Tallahassee.

To his wife, from East Carolina University, Greenville, N.C.,
September, 1962.

Dear Hon,

. . . So I slept late this morning, went down town and ate breakfast, then got prepared for my class, taking a shower and dressing, etc., even getting up notes as to what I would talk about—all of which later seemed to be a waste of time as it turned out I had only seven damned uninteresting students who hardly know what they are doing in the course. None of them the least bit interested in literature, writing or any of the rest of it. Not one of them had ever read anything of Thomas Wolfe, Hemingway, Faulkner; I don't think they really knew who they are. Actually, I asked around and [not] one of them would admit to even hearing of them. About all they seemed interested in was how I graded. One of them finally suggested that being as I was a writer more than a teacher I might even grade harder than somebody else. By this time I was a little fed up and told him I probably would. So I expect him to start changing courses by Monday. . . .

One bright thing in the day though was that I ran into Dave downtown, and he asked me to go hunting with him tomorrow. Going out for doves. I hope it works out; he'll call me in the morning.

I love you all, Mac

To Max Steele, from Greenville, N.C., November 9, 1962.

Dear Max,

. . . I am up here teaching now and the people are very literary and intelligent, and I have no one to communicate with. How about dropping me a note sometimes.

This teaching, I don't know whether I am cut out for it or

not. I got this place through John Ehle; * the president of the college talks like and looks like and acts like a Hollywood talent agent, . . . and he said I could teach here and that he had great ideas in mind that I could set up all these extension courses in writing and find some of this hidden talent in these little towns around Greenville. Well, I know enough to know there's not that much hidden talent hidden around in these little towns, and it also occurred to me that I didn't really care if it was—it could stay hidden as far as I was concerned—so I called him back and told him that I couldn't in clear conscience, take the job of digging this hidden talent out of those old women who wrote a poem thirty years ago. So he said to hell with that; it didn't really make any difference to him one way or the other—why didn't I just come up and teach anyhow? I said, "Teach what?" and he said it didn't make any difference what, just whatever I decided. "You're the teacher," he said. "*You* decide what to teach." So I thought about it and couldn't think of a damned thing I wanted to teach. So I rode up and talked with Ovid Pierce † and talked with Gwendolyn, and then it came to me that you couldn't ask for a much better job than a job in which you didn't have to do anything unless you wanted to, and not even that if it suited you, so I didn't figure I could beat it, and finally called back and took the thing. I know it sounds like a lie, but that is exactly the way it happened. I finally insisted on teaching something, and the president was a little irritated about it, but finally agreed to let me teach American literature. So that's what I'm doing now.

Do you know anything about this place? It's got six thousand students, bigger than Duke. It's kind of boomed in the

* An administrative assistant and adviser to Terry Sanford, then Governor of North Carolina. Ehle has written several novels, the last two being *The Road* and *The Landbreakers*.

† Ovid Williams Pierce, Duke '32, is the author of *The Plantation, On a Lonesome Porch,* and *The Devil's Half.* He is writer-in-residence at East Carolina University.

last few years, mainly according to this president, I think. He's damned interested in getting the place known. He's hired a new football coach and now is trying to get into the Southern Conference, and he is all wrapped up in building up the biggest symphony orchestra in the South. He called me the other day and said we got to get some damned fiddle players down here. It seems he's been scouting all over the state for good fiddle players and can't find any. . . . He's a real bug on that. Another thing he's a bug on is the new football stadium. He's going to open it next year with a bang by playing Wake Forest because "that'll get all the Baptist's support." I've suggested that instead we try to get the return bout of Liston and Patterson to open it which really would get national recognition, but nothing has come of that. . . .

How'd you like teaching? I can't quite make it out. At first I'd go in there and talk like a mad-man as hard as I could go for what seemed like four hours, covering everything from Aristotle to Faulkner, until I was hoarse and exhausted, and then would look at my watch and see that I had killed about fifteen minutes, and see all those faces staring at me in what I have since decided was a kind of horror, and then almost panic. So I went around getting tips on teaching methods, talked with Ovid Pierce (do you know him?) and learned such things as how to spend fifteen minutes calling the roll, five or ten minutes letting windows up and down, another fifteen minutes or so talking about the next days assignment, so that I can now spend almost the whole damned hour without even mentioning the subject. Ovid says when he runs down he just goes over and stares out the window for awhile. The students, he says, think he's thinking. He says with concentration he can stand there staring out for as long as ten minutes sometimes. He says it makes the students nervous as hell. Anyhow, I haven't been able to manage that yet. I just don't have that kind of confidence, I don't think.

Actually I don't communicate with them too well somehow. It took me a week before I could get anybody in the class to admit they had even heard of Thomas Wolfe. The fact of the matter is, I think, that a lot of them really haven't. But I get along with them some better now. We kill time together.

Don't know whether or not I'm going to stay here. I haven't brought the family up yet as nothing seems quite permanent. I've been going back and forth.

Not doing any writing to amount to anything. Ed Loessin is here; he's head of the drama department.

Later.

Was interrupted writing this the other night. One thing I wanted to ask you was whether or not you had read [Joseph Heller's] *Catch 22*. I just got around to it lately and was very much impressed. It also seemed to me over and over that this book was almost written for you as a reader, that it was right down your alley, so to speak. So if you haven't read it, I reccommennd (got enough double letters in that, I think.) [it] highly.

Went over to Durham this last week end to see the Tech-Duke game and spent the evening with Blackburn. He is about the same. Saw the slides of the trip we took to Greece, which he enjoys showing and which I enjoy seeing along with the lecture he gives. Second time I've seen them.

Working a little off and on, but nothing particularly exciting. Give regards to Diana and everybody.

Sincerely, Mac

To Max Steele, from Cordele, February 7, 1963.

Dear Max,

Thanks for the letter. I hadn't heard from you in so long that I was afraid I had said or written or done something that irritated your even and happy-go-lucky disposition, and I was —as you say Blackburn usually is—all ready to bite my tongue out.

Speaking of B., I received your letter in Greenville (where I am not now—I am in Cordele now; going to Florida tomorrow.) just after getting back from New York where I had been in order to appear on a TV show called "Meet the Professor" * with Blackburn (he was the prof. being honored) with Styron, Reynolds Price, and another fellow from Duke by the name of Fred Chappell who has a book coming out soon.† It was kind of fun in a way; they paid the expenses so we stayed at the Plaza and lived elegantly. It was to be one of the cultural things, a kind of impromptu discussion that Blackburn kept trying to plan in detail. "I'll say this to you and then you say that." We went through two hours of that kind of rehersal the day before and it got worse and worse and Blackburn got more and more nervous. (He had called me three times giving me exactly the same information—once all the way from New York to Greenville.) Everybody would chit-chat and nobody would take his planning seriously. Then the TV men would try to explain how they wanted it, and this would embarrass him. They wanted to show him as the good professor with us saying nice things about him. They wanted to show we were all friends. Blackburn would say he didn't see any sense in saying things like that. "The mere fact that we are all sitting here," he would say, "shows that we are getting along. I don't see any point in mentioning things like that." Instead, he wanted to discuss *high school* teachers who

* ABC Television, Sunday, February 3, 1963.

† William Styron, Duke '47, is the author of *Lie Down In Darkness*, *The Long March*, *Set This House on Fire*, and *The Confessions of Nat Turner* (Pulitzer Prize, 1967); Reynolds Price, Duke '55, author of *A Long and Happy Life* (Faulkner Foundation Award, 1962), *The Names and Faces of Heroes*, *A Generous Man*, and *Love and Work*, is an associate professor of English at Duke; and Fred Chappell, Duke '61, author of *It Is Time, Lord*, *The Inkling*, and *Dagon*, is an associate professor of English at the University of North Carolina, Greensboro.

influenced us as writers and the theory that most writers had had lonely child-hoods between the ages of thirteen and about sixteen during which period they did a lot of reading. I told him that I personally didn't care to sit on TV with a bunch of people watching and discuss my lonely childhood. All the others agreed with this, and Blackburn pouted. Reynolds wanted to discuss the time that he (Blackburn) threw a chair at one of the students. The TV people didn't like this line, and finally Blackburn came up with the notion that we discuss the way writers become *aware* of things. He mentioned Styron's great feeling for water and things like that. I said I thought that would be embarrassing too. If Willie wanted to discuss how he became aware of water, it would be all right, but I didn't want to discuss things like that. Blackburn began to get right miserable. And the more miserable he got, the happier everybody was.

Did you see it by any chance? It was on last Sunday. I haven't seen it myself. Actually, it went off all right. We went down the next day and they taped about forty-five minutes of profound discussion with the idea of trimming it down later, and I believe it worked all right. Blackburn and Styron carried the ball most of the way, and we chit-chatted all right. We got off on one or two kind of silly subjects. One of them was how young writers are influenced by other writers and whether or not they were influenced too much and whether or not it was a good idea to read (this was after the subject began running away with us) to read good writers or not, and we went on about this until we reached the dead-end of the whole question which unfortunately ended with me so that I came out with the bright remark: "Well, if you are not going to read [good] writers, who are you going to read?" which I thought was bright at the time, but suddenly succeeded, I thought, in making all of us—me especially—look kind of silly. Anyhow, we dropped that then and went on to some more impromptu profundity.

I didn't teach at Greenville this quarter and don't much think I will. I wasn't too good at it. And I didn't do any writing worth doing so I decided it probably wasn't worth it. I wrote about half a screen-play and a synopsis for the rest, but it was real junk. So I've come home and now trying to think of what to do next, outside of writing.

I'm not even going [to] ask you what you are going to do with a nineteen room house.* I'm not even going to ask you that. . . .

I'm sorry to hear you are not going on through with the novel. I'm sure—absolutely sure somehow—that you are under-rating it and probably being too hard on it. Is anybody that you can trust reading it as you go along? But I know what you mean by putting it aside. I remember when I was in the Air Force the last time and I would get too carried away with writing and would realize that it was making my life miserable somehow, I would make it a point to take everything I had—typewriter and all—and put it in the closet and say to hell with it. I would say to it: "All right, stay there, you bastard. You're going to stay there until it is understood that I'm in control of this situation, not you. You're not running my life or ruining it either—I'm the writer and I'm running you, and until that's understood, you stay there." Then I'd leave it in there, feeling strong and powerful, and I wouldn't take it back out again until it was properly punished for presuming to be too much. It worked sometimes too. That was when I was doing some fairly decent writing, though.

Myself, I've decided I'm not going to write any more junk. I've tried writing junk, and it falls below that level. If I try to write good stuff, I at least come up with acceptable junk. Aim at a poem and settle for a novel, as they say.

Had better stop as it is late and I've had several drinks and might get profound. Give my regards to everybody and let me

* The Steeles had bought a large house, which was divided into three apartments, as an investment.

hear from you. I'm not going to ask you what you are going to do with a nineteen room house.

As ever, Mac

P.S. *14 Feb.* Went to Fla. without mailing this. Just got back.

M.

To William Blackburn, from Cordele, April 10, 1963.

Dear Dr. Blackburn,

Many thanks for the copy of the book, and of course for including my story in it.* I'm proud to have it there. . . .

Right now am half-way thinking about going out to California this summer if things work out. They're planning on doing a TV series out of NTFS and I might possibly go out and work on it. I really don't care too much about it, but I do nothing much around here but play golf and poker, and it would probably be better to be doing some writing than no writing at all, no matter what it is. I've said that often, though, but once I get down to it, I can't quite stick it. I frankly don't get much satisfaction or pleasure out of TV stuff, despite the money, and think it pretty much a waste of time if I don't enjoy it. However, I would like to do a good movie if I could and this might possibly be one way of working into it.

Anyhow, because of that, I think probably I'm going to hold off on trying to get anything to do up at Duke for awhile.† Actually, I really would like a job very much of some sort, but I don't care much about a job that has anything to do with writing. I don't know why; it just seems to bother me somehow. I'd much prefer to have a job in which I worked

---

* "The Dove Shoot," in *Under 25: Duke Narrative and Verse, 1945–1962* (Durham, 1963).

† Since Hyman had expressed a desire to live in Durham, I had suggested the possibility of his applying for a job in public relations at Duke.

with people in something completely divorced from writing and do any writing I might do on the side, more as a hobby than anything else, and never depend on it at all for anything. To do nothing but write is a deadly and boring life to me, and for some reason or other, it makes me feel like a bum. To write junk—either commercial junk or literary junk (and there is plenty of that around too)—also makes me feel like a bum. I don't like having to depend either on a buying public or critics; I particularly don't care for the idea of trying to cater to either one of them for my well-being—either financial, psychological, or any other way. So I think I would probably be better off in some other kind of work so I could write what I wanted to when I wanted to without regard to anything or anybody except what makes me feel good to write. Of course that is the ideal situation, but I think to get close to it at all, I'm going to have to find something else to do. I know that TV is not the answer, but that is something you can always quit and walk off from. At least, I have done it before.

We enjoyed seeing you. What are you going to do this summer? I hope your plans are more definite than mine. If you feel like roaming around and we're still here, we'd be glad to have you down this way. I'll take you fishing, golfing and poker playing. That's fun too, but too much of that can make you feel like a bum too, I've found out.

Thanks again for the book.

As ever, Mac

Mac Hyman died of a massive heart attack on the evening of July 17, 1963. Within the hour he had completed arrangements by telephone to go to Hollywood the next day to work on television sketches from No Time for Sergeants. *He is buried in Cordele.*